Sexpectations:
Women Talk Candidly
about Sex and Dating

Sexpectations:
Women Talk Candidly about Sex and Dating

Printed in the United States of America

10 9 8 7 6 5 4 3 2

Contents

Disclaimer

This book explores many risky and controversial sexual activities. Readers should not attempt any of the activities described in these pages without full knowledge of the hazards inherent. Neither the author of this book, nor its interviewees, nor its publisher assume any responsibility for the use or misuse of the practices described herein.

People involved in bondage, discipline and sadomasochism (BDSM) are well aware of the hazards inherent in what they do and take care to anticipate them, to understand them, and to avoid them.

People involved in BDSM make a real and absolute distinction between explicitly consensual acts between adult partners for their mutual pleasure and all of acts of violence against unconsenting partners. Imposing any sexual activity on an unwilling partner (or upon anyone who cannot give legal consent) is a criminal offense. Further, state laws vary: Some of these activities, even between consenting partners, are illegal in certain jurisdictions.

Acknowledgements

I gratefully acknowledge the people have stood by me during this project, no matter what: Roan Kaufman, Murray K., Dmitri, Tony Jarvis, and my family.

Constant support and inspiration: Roy Schenk, without whom this book would not be possible, Craig Rypstat, Erin Farwell, Mailee Hunt, Geoffrey Goodridge, Samurai, Roni Raye, Beverlee Couliard, TMLP-Heartland, Lauren Hambrook, David Lasker, Boyles, Bethanne, Lee, Sara M., Eric Pierson, Jerry Courzo, and Asa Baber.

This book is dedicated to the memory of Ravi Dutta.

Introduction

Sex, sex, sex! It possesses the male mind. At least it has possessed mine. What guy do you know who doesn't obsess about sex, at least sometimes? What you might not know is that many women obsess about sex, too. They just hide it better than most guys.

Since I was 14, I have wondered what women thought about, desired and craved in sex. What are women's deepest and darkest fantasies? What do they want that they are too afraid to share? I have talked about it, joked about it, and read about it, but rarely have I heard from women, themselves, about what they enjoy.

I wrote *Sexpectations* as a quest to understand the "secret" world of women. In the process, I wanted to give women an opportunity to express themselves for both men and women to read.

This book is about women's sexual experiences and desires, told in women's own words. It reads as if you were there with me, talking to the women, asking them whatever you've always wanted to know—but may have been afraid to ask. It is an opportunity to hear women explain what they look for on a romantic date, how it feels to be tied up, what it's like to be a professional phone sex operator, and much more.

Sexpectations spans many realms. We learn what women want from men on romantic dates, and we hear the graphic sexual

1

experiences of professional dominatrixes. Many of the women are interested in bondage, discipline (B&D) and sadomasochism (S/M). This book documents conversations with some of the most intense women I've ever met.

One woman likes to be stuffed into a wooden box so that only her head sticks out, then forced into sex with her "master." Another woman just loves to hold hands. The women in the book represent all levels of sexual experience. The women range in age from 19 to 57, and their occupations run the gamut from fast food cashiers to corporate lawyers. The women interviewed were mostly from the U.S., from small towns in Kentucky to New York and Los Angeles. I also interviewed many women in Canada and a few from England.

The interviews are a gateway into the secret world of women. It provides access to women's fantasies, stories, opinions, advice, and troubles. The book is intended to be fun, useful, meaningful, and humorous. Let it stimulate your thoughts and desires. Conclusions, if there can be any, are for you to draw. This book is merely a diving board into the pool of sex. It offers the promise of a satisfying sex life that is generated from the freedom to dream.

With that, I present *Sexpectations*.

Chapter 1: The Girls Next Door

Roni Raye Productions

Chapter 1: The Girls Next Door
Age 19–35

This chapter focuses on women between the ages of 19 and 35. We might call them "the young and restless." We might remember them as "the girls next door."

When young, beautiful women walk down the street, they are often the ones who catch men's eyes. They radiate sexual energy. These youthful women are still exploring their sexuality and their fantasy lives. They are ready to blossom in their sexuality. They are still discovering what they like and dislike, and what they want in a partner. They express a sense of innocence, curiosity, and willingness to explore.

Many of the "girls next door" may seem bland on the outside, but they can be surprisingly sexy inside. Most escape our glance, blend into the background, and disappear into the sea of faces we see each day. They may not immediately grab our attention, but on closer examination turn out to be the deep ones. They often have a wildly passionate and intense private life.

The point of this chapter is to give these younger women, the girls next door, room to express themselves. The women in this chapter represent many sexual categories. They discuss dating, romance, extreme sex, and their desires like no other age group.

Name:	**Dee Dee**
Age:	**23**
Occupation:	**Student**
Relationship Status:	**In a committed relationship**

Describe a wonderful date you've been on. What happened?
We invited another woman out with us because we have a flavor for that, threesomes and so forth.

Did you know her ahead of time?
We met her a couple weeks before at another gathering at a gay bar. We went out to a restaurant and ate and then we went back to a mixed bar and did a little drinking and dancing. We got lots of stares from other people; that was interesting.

You were attracted to this woman when you met her? Had you been with other women before her?
Yes, I was very attracted to her when we met, and no, I hadn't been with other women before her.

Were you nervous about meeting her?
Extremely.

How old is she?
She is 19. We were robbing the cradle. The age of consent in Canada is only 16.

Did you plan ahead of time to have sex with her?
We didn't know for sure ahead of time. She wanted to experience it and I wanted to experience it. We invited her out and told her that if she was uncomfortable she could sleep on the hideaway bed, because she had come in from out of town. In the end we all chose to get together.

What happened on the date? I feel like a guy on a dating show asking about the details.

It was just like a regular date. We all went out for supper, then went back to the bar, and then came home. Do I have to tell you the intimate details?

You can tell me as much or as little as you want. However, my readers want to know every detail. At what point during the date did you know that you were going to be sexual with her?

Probably when the three of us were dirty dancing. We kissed on the dance floor and I was getting turned on. We had talked before about what we all wanted to do and what we hoped would happen.

What is your sex life like now?

Our sex life goes around B&D and slight S/M.

Are you a top or a bottom?

Both, we interchange it.

How long have you been experimenting with BDSM?

For about six months.

How did you start?

I think it started with asphyxiation, strangling, and then it went to rope, just four corners of the bed tying up.

How did you start with asphyxiation? What was it like?

He placed his hands around my neck and restricted my breathing somewhat.

It sounds like before this you were totally vanilla and that seems like a huge jump. How did you make the transition?

We were having sex and he put his hands around my neck. It was the first time I had ever had anyone do that. It was just

7

lightly done, nothing serious. I think I put my hands over his hands and told him to go tighter.

Were you surprised that you were into it? Did it freak you out?

Yes, I was surprised that I liked it so much. It didn't quite freak me out because my partner was quite calm about everything, and because he didn't react it kept me calm.

What went through your head when he started grabbing your neck?

The first thing I thought was how surprising it was that I was enjoying it. Then I just threw that out of my head and went with it. It was very orgasmic for me. Later we started to experiment with tying each other up. We were tree planting and we bought rope in one of the nearby small towns.

So while you were planting trees, did you do this experimentation in your tent?

Yeah, we tied hands and feet together. It was relaxing.

What is one of your favorite sexual scenarios?

I like the mail bag. We have a big canvas mail bag we stuff each other in. We stuff each other inside. I've been hung up while I am inside.

What is it like to be hung up while inside it?

You are totally free and swing around. You are totally disoriented. I get hung up from the door frame. I usually don't like to be left for too long. Most times around five to ten minutes. Sometimes he laughs at me when I am hanging there.

What is your darkest fantasy?

I think the darkest is when I am on top of him. When I dominate, I am really into it. It is a little scary for me because I am so into it. I know I still hold back some because I am a little worried.

What might happen if you fully let go?
I might gag him too long and choke him, or even kill him.

What is your advice for men who just want to have one night stands?
I once watched a guy go around a whole bar, going up to every woman saying, "It's my birthday. Will you fuck me?" By the end of the evening he got it. It's the only time I've ever seen a guy do something to make sure he got fucked. Some women were grossed out by him, he got slapped, he got drinks poured on him, but he kept going. Finally he left with a woman. I watched him the whole night and the woman he left with was not that bad looking.

If you are only looking for a one night stand, it is best to go to a cheap bar, usually with young people. Bring lots of money and buy lots of drinks for women. Probably invite not only her, but her friends back to a place where there is more alcohol. From there something will usually happen. I would tell a guy to go to bar with lots of drunk women. Take the path of least resistance.

Name:	Alexandra
Occupation:	Tech support for an internet server
Age:	23
Relationship Status:	Engaged

Where do you generally meet the guys you date?
Most of the men I've dated I've met through swingers magazines and personals ads. There are many magazines in my area. There have only been two people I've dated in the past three years who I didn't meet through ads. The reason I prefer guys I meet through ads is because I get to know them before meeting them. I get the chance to really get to know them before I actually see them. I get a better first impression.

Over the past few years I have been going through a period of sexual exploration. For a while I wanted to be with as many men as possible. I wanted to experiment with couples, other girls, and men of all ages. Placing ads provided me with many men I wouldn't normally come into contact with, especially older men.

Is monogamy essential to you?
Not really. Right now, I'm bisexual and so is my fiancé. We've told each other as far as the opposite sex goes, we're monogamous, but his bisexuality and my bisexuality is a part of us that the other cannot fulfill. As long as we're open about it and don't go doing it behind each other's backs, that is fine with us. I am not the jealous type. If my boyfriend wanted to sleep with another woman it would be fine with me. I miss the variety of sleeping with other men.

Would you consider having an affair?
I certainly would. I already have slept with a few women; my
boyfriend knew about that. If I had an opportunity I couldn't
pass up with another guy; I would go for it.

What was the oldest guy you've had sex with?
During my period of intense dating; I slept with several men
in their 40's, and a few in their 50's. I loved their confidence
and their patience with me. It was great to have them take
me out and buy gifts for me. The older men would always
shower me with gifts and compliments.

Have you had many one night stands in your life?
Yes, many. I'm not proud of it.

What is an approximate number?
At least 40. I feel so bad about it. When I look back on my
time of dating tons of guys, I just feel dirty.

*I don't think you are bad or wrong. You were just experimenting.
More women should give themselves that freedom. Where did you
meet the guys you were having one night stands with?*
Once again, most of them I met through ads. There were a
bunch I met through ads who were just in town for the
night. We would just get to talking and decide we would go
out or whatever, we'd go out and do the deed, and that
would be it.

*What was it about them that made you comfortable enough to sleep
with them in such a quick period of time?*
A lot of the people I knew already. They had written me
letters and we had talked on the phone. To be quite honest,
for probably six months I would sleep with just about
anybody. I was very promiscuous. Once again, I am not
proud of what happened. I never thought about the

repercussions. I just did it for sex. I knew it was just going to be a one night stand. All I wanted was something different for the night. I wanted to experience as many men as possible.

How could I get you into bed tonight?

There are many important things you can do. For starters, make me laugh. If you can make me truly laugh more than once in a night either on purpose or accidentally, that is a real turn-on. Also, if you can look me in the eye and show some genuine interest in what I say and really listen when I say something and really hear it, then there is an attraction. If you do any of these things well, there is a pretty good chance it will happen, as long as that person makes the first move. I very rarely make the first move as far as sex goes. I am more submissive. But if I want a guy to make the first move I will touch his arm, look him in the eyes, and sit close to him.

What can guys do to get laid?

I think a lot of women want someone who will listen to them. Women sometimes want to cry on a man's shoulder and have him say, "Poor baby," and sound like he means it. That goes really far with women. If you can pour a couple of drinks down her throat, all the better.

What do you wear if you want to turn on a man?

I love lingerie and I have quite an extensive collection of it. I have everything from little nightgowns to teddies that could be used for eye patches. As for other clothes, I have a lot of silk, the button-up silk shirts that I can wear a thin slip shirt underneath and have it open so guys can see me. I have high heels and short skirts for when I am going out and actively trying to find somebody. I have a section of my closet for short skirts and a section of long skirts for work and when I go to see my family.

Do you enjoy giving pain?

I don't like beating the shit out of people. There is a certain point when pain becomes pain. The kind of pain I like is running my nails down somebody's back, maybe a little hair-pulling, biting not enough to draw blood, the things you do out of passion. I don't mind a guy restraining me when we are in the heat of the moment, or leaving bite marks on me. I love sex, and I love the passion involved.

What are the three stages of sex?

There is fucking, there is having sex, and there is making love. Fucking is what you can do with anybody. Sex is what you do with someone you like and there is the potential for having deep feelings. Making love is with the person you want to spend the rest of your life with. That is spiritual for me.

Name:	**Carrie**
Age:	**30**
Occupation:	**Clerk in a law firm**
Relationship Status:	**Single**

What do you consider romantic?

It is not so much a specific gesture. Most people wouldn't even call it romantic, but I prefer a guy who will go to movies and do things that I like as well as what he likes. A guy who is willing to hang out with my friends and their children, or with my family, not always guy stuff all the time. Flowers are nice, but if I want them I can go buy them. I like sensitivity, like when a man takes into account what I like. Sensitivity is more romantic than someone who buys me lots of things but doesn't care as much.

If a man approached you in the grocery store or some other public place and asked you out, would you consider going out with him?

I am a pretty laid back person. I would probably go out with a guy unless he did something that scares me, like being strange, being extremely forward, or saying suggestive things to me. If he isn't scary, I would probably be willing to meet him in a public place. I wouldn't give him my phone number or tell him where I live, but I would take his phone number and meet him sometime.

However, the kind of guy I would respond to in the grocery store would not come up and immediately hit on me. It is a cliché, but if I was shopping and we just started chatting about food or whatever, then I would be interested. If it was conversational and it was clear that he wasn't just out scoping, then I would be more likely to be interested in him.

How would you respond in this situation: You are out on a date and you like the guy pretty much. Let's say it is the second date, and you want to sleep with him. What kind of signals do you give him to tell him you are interested?

I tend to be a very submissive person in relationships with men. When I am interested in someone, I tend to do whatever I think they want.

Are you attracted to powerful men?

Very much so. I equate power with success. I view success not in terms of money, but in terms of accomplishing goals, someone who does what he wants. I define powerful not in terms of being the owner of a company or something like that, but powerful because he has power over his own life. I am also very attracted to men who are intelligent.

Do you have one night stands?

Yes, I do. It happens maybe once a month.

Where do you meet these guys?

I meet them at clubs, bars or through friends. When I meet someone, I know if I would consider sleeping with him or not; that happens pretty much instantaneously. If I meet a guy who is moderately obnoxious and a little bit cocky, but very nice looking, I would probably sleep with him as soon as he made a pass. If I found him attractive and he made a move, I would definitely take him up on it.

So if he was very intelligent and personable, but average looking, would you also sleep with him?

Intellectual men are a big turn-on. I would probably still sleep with him. If I wasn't looking for a one night stand, I would wait until I got to know the guy much better. But I know myself well enough to know that once I've decided whether I would sleep with someone ever; I would probably sleep with him on the first night.

What is a typical first move on you?

I never make the first move. Typically I meet a guy in a public place and we go someplace else, not his house, but some place that is semi-public, like a restaurant. Usually, he doesn't make the first move until 3:00 a.m. when things are winding down. He either asks if I want to come to his house, or if he can give me a ride. Sometimes they ask if they can come over to my house. Occasionally guys ask me if I want to get coffee. The best one is, "I've had too much to drink. I better not drive. Can you give me a ride?" That is a good one because it shows intelligence in the guy. Most guys wouldn't admit that they have had too much to drink.

What is the fastest way to get you into bed?

The fastest way is to be gorgeous and smart. I don't know why, but when someone tells me he is a lawyer, that is a big brownie point right there. I would probably be in bed with a lawyer within a half an hour of meeting him. He would have to be very bright and very attractive. I think the fastest way to get me in bed is to be intelligent and able to converse with me, and not try to get me in bed.

What do men in general need to know if they want to have one night stands?

I don't quite know how to answer that, because it is hard to know what a guy doesn't know until you've been with him. It is like the old cliché thing, after I have a one night stand with a guy he sprints out the door at 3:00 or 4:00 a.m., or if I am at his place, he rattles me around 6:00 a.m., and wants me out of there before daybreak. I find those men very annoying. I understand it is a one night stand, but if it is a Friday night, I don't want to be rattled out of bed and kicked out the door at 6:00 a.m.

Do you like men to be very aggressive in sex?

When it comes to sex, I am very submissive. I like a lot of things. I like to be tied up; it happens occasionally. A lot of people like to be tied up, so that is common, but going beyond that is rare. I've only had one guy spank me and I like that.

What would be the ultimate dominance/submission play for you?

A guy making me have sex with another guy while he is there. I dated a police officer for a while. He was the first guy who was into anything more than standard dominance. He was very aggressive in terms of liking to do what he liked to do. He was a police officer, so he would bring out his handcuffs. He worked at night from 11:00 p.m. until 7:00 a.m. I didn't see him that often because our schedules conflicted. I would see him on the weekends or in the evenings from 6:00 p.m. until 10:00 p.m.

One night he came over with another police officer. He wanted me to have sex with the other police officer while he watched. It took a lot of convincing because I had never done anything like that before. I had never even considered it before then, but it was fun.

The one thing about that police officer is that he always talked; it was just never ending. He liked to receive oral sex, but he didn't like to give it. His mouth was always busy talking unless we were kissing.

He liked to handcuff me to the head of the bed and pretend he was ordering me around. His friends would watch us have sex and he would tell me what he wanted me to do.

Do you like giving up power and control for a while during sex?

Yes, I do. It happened a few times with the police officer; he did it quite a few times. He once brought four of his friends over, but I wouldn't do anything. I remember one of the first times he brought a friend over, I was so mad. He was a really good guy, funny, large and attractive. I felt so angry, like he put me between a rock and a hard place. He knew I had never done anything like that before and he completely put me on the spot. He wanted to be in complete control; that was just the way he was. Over time, I had sex with several of his friends.

What is it about being submissive that brings you joy?
I like to do things for others that I know brings them pleasure. Most men really enjoy getting a blow-job and it took me a long time to be willing to do that, never mind do it without them asking. It took me a long time to enjoy doing it. I enjoy doing it because guys love it. They prefer that over most other things. I like to do something that pleases someone else so much. The joy of being submissive is that the person being dominant enjoys it.

Name:	**Theresa**
Age:	**27**
Occupation:	**Teacher**
Relationship Status:	**Single**

Have you ever slept with other teachers or parents of students?
Yes, I slept with a principal once. I also slept with a teachers aide. With the teachers aide, there had been a lot of flirting and talking and hanging out together after school for a long time. I knew he wanted me. So I just taunted and teased him for a while and finally decided to give in.

Did you fuck him on a school desk or what?
No, and I don't find that funny.

Was he older than you?
Yea, probably 15 years older. The other guy was a principal. We had known each other for almost a year. We worked in the same office and we were just really friendly, but no attraction or flirting at all. Then we were together at a teachers convention and afterwards we all went to a bar. He started flirting with me and the attraction became obvious. Then he gave me his phone number and told me to call him, which I did. We went out for a drink and went back to my house and kissed vigorously.

He was a married man, wasn't he?
Yes, he was. Then on the next date we did the nasty.

What does it take to get you into bed?
It takes a lot of flirting and knowing that there is interest. I am not usually looking to chase someone or have a big conquest. I don't go for someone unless I know there is interest. I am very forward and most people I want to sleep with I do. I like it when I get to seduce someone.

19

What do men need to know to have one night stands with women?
Men do lots of stupid things. They try to show off for
women with their achievements. Being obvious is not
attractive at all. To be overly bragging is another turn off.
Guys need to be smooth and suave and have a sharp wit.

What does "suave" mean to you?
Men who are suave don't have that hesitant young boy type
of thing. They are like Cassanova. They just say things that
turn you on.

*So a boy is going to be fishing around for things to say and a suave
guy knows what to do? At the same time, a suave guy is kind of
manipulative, is that correct?*
Yea, but it's okay to be manipulative. I am manipulative. I
don't want to have to teach some young guy how to be sexy
or how to please me. I don't want someone to fumble
around. I like guys who are aggressive.

*Then why do the pouty tortured artist types get so much attention
from women?*
I have no idea. Maybe when you go out with a guy like that
it seems like you will have more power or control because
they are not suave. I like power and control.

What is the fastest way to get you into bed tonight?
If you are not shy or intimidated about physical contact, that
gives me a sign that in bed you will be that way. A "nice guy"
wouldn't be as confident being physical in public.

Name:	**Shannah**
Age:	**25**
Occupation:	**Magazine Editorial Assistant**
Relationship Status:	**Has a boyfriend**

What qualities do you look for in the men you date?

I look for men with self-confidence, intelligence and self-possessiveness. I want a man who is sure of who he is and his own ideas, not looking around for what to believe in and be about. Guys who don't know what they are about tend to be easily influenced. They are often looking for a woman to sexually define them somehow. I am not attracted to that at all. I am attracted to someone who is really skilled at what he is doing or is really sure about what he is doing.

What signals do you give a guy when you are interested in him?

I joke a lot and use humor. If I am interested in the guy I will be very excited inside. I am a very happy person, and I flirt right off the bat. I don't flirt in a real obvious way, but I tease them or whatever.

If you are not interested in a guy, will you be more reserved?

Yes. If I am not interested in a guy, I will be more reserved and not encourage any conversation.

Is romance important to you?

Yes, it is very important to me. Romance is someone showing signs that he is interested in me. He can show me he's interested by calling me or responding over and above the call of duty. One way he can show he is interested is by paying for the date when we go out. Where I come from it is so Dutch all the time that it is nice to be taken out. I like the old fashioned romantic things, having him do those little gestures. Doing small things is romantic and that means the guy is interested in me. Although, it shouldn't be overly done, it should be subtle. Otherwise, I feel as though I owe him something.

Don't you think that is confusing for the guy?
Yes, it is very confusing. Guys need to use their intuition a lot more, but they also need to talk to the girl a lot. All this stuff I am saying can all be done through talking. I think if you are just generous and you go with your affection, the women may misread your affection, but she won't be upset.

Why do you want the men you are dating to be confused and not clear about what you expect from him? Being confused and getting mixed messages from a woman drives me nuts. It creates a situation where I can't win or please her. Could you consider giving the guy a break and really being straight with him about what you want?
No. I completely disagree. Men need to listen to their intuition much more. Men often go overboard with me, without listening to what I want. They try to impress me and come on too strong. Men need to quit the game playing and listen more. I don't care if I am confusing!

Do you date men who are significantly older or younger than you are?
My boyfriend is 45. I always date men who are older than me, usually men at least 30. Men my age [25] don't appeal to me.

Do you go out of your way to find older men?
I think it's the crowd I hang with. Older men tend to be the more self-possessed confident ones; that's certainly been my experience.

When you walk down the street, are the older guys the ones you check out?

It's not that I am checking them out; they tend to check me out. Guys my own age tend to be much more shy than older guys. The guys who actually go out of their way to introduce themselves or make small talk standing in the coffee line in the cafe, they are not younger guys, they are older guys. So that's who I end up being with.

When you are out and about and a guy approaches you, what do you think?

If he's cute, I will be much more interested than if he is not cute. Cuteness has to do with charm, the way you approach someone. Physical appearance is also important, and the way you present yourself.

If you met a guy and he asked you to go on a to date sometime, what would you say?

It is important to be specific. Someone has to be interesting to grab my attention. "Would you like to date sometime?" totally doesn't turn me on.

Has your desire for sex changed over time?

No, I am still very lustful all the time. I am very horny all the time. One thing about the guy that I'm dating is that he is so busy we only have sex three or four times a week and I would like to have it every night. I've toned it down. I am lustful, but I don't go acting it out, out of respect for our relationship.

What would it take for you to have an affair?

I might be having an affair with a woman very soon, but he is okay with that. I used to cheat on boyfriends, that's why I always called them lovers. They couldn't be boyfriends because I wanted an open relationship.

How many people have you slept with?

Twenty-five.

What issues come up for you around one night stands?

Sex for women is a lot more wrapped up with the emotions than it is for guys. So when a woman just wants to get laid, sure, she can just get laid, but it is really hard not to get tangled up in the emotional consequences of that one night stand. She might feel terrible. Men don't seem to have that problem. For me, I tend to have all these feelings for a guy after I sleep with him. Before I open my body to them, I feel confident and flirty and outgoing. Afterward, I feel so vulnerable. I even get all clingy on the guy. I feel unstable until I get the response from the guy that he cares for me.

Do you have rape fantasies?

Yes, I do. In my fantasies there are a lot of guys, and they totally humiliate me. They rip off my clothes, hold me down and expose parts of my body in public places. I fantasize about all sorts of nasty stuff.

Do you think about this fantasy a lot?

Whenever I masturbate. Sometimes my boyfriend and I act out parts. I get really excited if he spanks me or holds my wrists down. If he uses any force I get very excited. My boyfriend is too gentle to really hurt me, but he will act out certain aggression, like holding me down. However, all the time he will be very gentle in his words because he is not a violent person.

In your fantasies would he humiliate you and verbally abuse you?

My fantasies are always about strangers, so my boyfriend is never in them. I don't fantasize about verbal abuse. In my fantasies, men would be restraining me, forcing me into embarrassing positions, like bending me over and ripping off my clothes. It is pretty bad. I like the idea of being out of control.

24

Name: **Ann**
Age: **25**
Occupation: **Restaurant manager**
Relationship Status: **Single**

What kind of men are you attracted to?

I've reached the point where I don't take a guy's phone number; I give him mine. If he is interested, he will actually call, and if he is too chickenshit and doesn't call, then I wouldn't want to go out with him anyway. I am really attracted to men with confidence, who know what they want and don't waffle. They are either kind of hard to find, or I am attracting all the ones that are not confident.

Why do you attract such wimpy men?

I think because I am a powerful woman and certain men are attracted to that and some are scared to death of it. It depends on the guy.

Are the men who are attracted to you also submissive?

I don't know why they are, because I don't get off on that at all. I really want them to have balls and tell me to shut up when I deserve it. I want men who are opinionated, not who do whatever I say, because that gets really old after a while. I make so many decisions in my life that it is really great to be with a man who will take charge and say, "This is what we are going to do tonight and you are going to enjoy it."

Have you gone out with guys like that?

Not yet, but he is on the horizon. I want a guy who can take charge at times, but I also want equal power. I don't think relationships should be one-sided; they should have the power shared between the two people. Also, it is important to empower the other person. If I am always in charge, I start getting annoyed. When they are always in charge, I start thinking they are a real prick. There needs to be a compromise.

How does a guy act when you feel he respects you?

That is a good question. I can tell when a guy respects me because he is honest with me, authentic, and he doesn't try to hide things from me. Also, when I say something, he doesn't put me down. He respects my opinion as much as I respect his opinion. When men are intimidated by me, they tend to skirt around and aren't honest and authentic. It is a total turn off.

I love to spoil my boyfriends and like to be spoiled in return. It doesn't have to be things that are bought, but just running his fingers through my hair and cuddling, the simple things.

What is wrong with a man being intimidated by a woman? It seems like it will eventually happen in regards to some issue in a relationship. It's a catch-22 for men, because women don't like it when men are weak, yet they want them to be honest and open all the time.

I also believe that everything can be resolved through communication, if you are willing. Resolution can come if you are willing to go past where you are stopped in communication. How can being open and honest be intimidating? All a guy has to do is tell me that he doesn't feel comfortable with something, and I will be the first to change for him.

What advice would you give men on dating: how to meet women, how to date, and how to act?

Stop being so significant and have fun with it. You may die tomorrow, so we might as well have a great night.

What do you mean by "significant"?

Guys get all caught up in whether or not they should talk to a girl. They get intimidated because they think she is very pretty, or they get wrapped up in whether or not they should ask her out. Guys tend to get significant and all wrapped up with themselves about whether or not they should even go up and talk to a girl. I would tell them to live juicy. Live juicy and enjoy it. Just go for it. Stop thinking about whether or not she is going to say no. She may say yes, you never know.

How can men learn to read women's body language? How can men learn when to approach a woman and when to go away?

For me, if I am interested in the guy enough and I want to get physical with him, I will start getting physical. I will put my hand on his knee, put my arm around his waist or put my arm through his arm. I will be very casual about it, but I will actually touch him. I might just grab him and kiss him.

What do you love about being pursued?

I love getting a card once a week or flowers for no special reason. I like a phone call or a message left on my answering machine like, "I just wanted to call and tell you I love you." For me, that is being courted. I love to know the man is thinking of me. I get butterflies in my stomach and I can't wait to see him. I can't wait to throw him in bed and pounce on him.

Is romance important to you?

Yes, it means coming home to a hot bubble bath and a man to wash my hair. It's flowers every now and then for a surprise. It's calling my voice mail to say he loves me, or a kiss and a hug for no reason. Romantic walks on the beach. Getting in the car and going on a surprise trip. Holding hands in the movies.

Why do men love courting and women love to be courted? And then when guys get the women, they often dump them. Is it just the chase they love?

I think it is a deep fear of commitment, and they love the conquest. If a guy is good at courting, and I am even slightly interested in him, I will be his within two weeks.

How do you bring romance to your relationships?

I give more than I expect in return. I am the first one to call his answering machine to tell him how much he means to me and acknowledge him for something he's done. I am always asking him if there is anything I can do to make his day easier. I love cooking dinner for him. I always offer to give him back rubs and I just give him tenderness. There is no beating around the bush, life is too short.

Do your friends or family ever set you up on dates?

My mother loves dating shows; she's been on all of them. She tells people about her single daughter when she is on them. She has been on "Love Connection." She told everyone about the tattoo on her boob on national TV. Chuck didn't know what to do with himself. He was flabbergasted.

My mother frequently tells me to go on a dating show. She is always giving me names of guys. She does the makeup for a show in my town. She tells guys that she has the most beautiful daughter and carries around a photograph of me. She tells me things like, "Call him before he is on the show because he will have so many women calling in." I get at least one name and phone number from her each week.

My mom is also a medical assistant. She gets numbers when guys come in to get their physical. She will tell me things about the man's health. She also does medical exams for insurance companies. She used to give out my phone number until I got upset with her. She was giving out my number to complete strangers.

At what point during the date do you know if you are going to sleep with him?
There is an element of cat and mouse about sex. For me, I end up having a little more control if we don't have sex. If we are making out and one thing leads to another, I am not going to stop it. I am not the one to have us lay in bed touching each other and then stop it. I am not a dick tease.

I am glad to hear that. What do you wear when you want to turn guys on?
I have quite big breasts and a somewhat small waist. I will usually wear something that enhances my chest, something that I feel sexy in. I like to wear a black bra and I usually don't wear undies. I usually have a couple of outfits that I love and I know I look great in them, so I'll wear those. I am not into lots of makeup or lace.

What qualities do you look for in a one night stand?
The man I want as a partner wouldn't be a one night stand type. I have never had a fuck buddy, because when I have sex with someone I become attached. I can't just have sex to have sex. To me, there has to be something more to it than just having sex. There has to be a level of commitment, trust and honesty with the other person that is unsurpassed by anything else.

I used to have one night stands when I was younger, between 18 and 23. I just don't do it anymore. In the morning, I would end up feeling even worse. Usually the only reason I would sleep with them was because I was just craving having someone else with me.

How do you fulfill that need now?
I just use my vibrator.

What do you think about when you masturbate?

I don't usually think about guys. I might masturbate while
reading a book or sometimes even while reading the
newspaper. I might just read a normal book, like Reader's
Digest. For me it is just a physical need.

I have had some great lovers and lousy lovers. The great
lovers were guys I would fantasize about, but I haven't had a
great lover for a few years. Now it is just a physical release. I
think the only time I masturbate about things like guys going
down on me is when I masturbate in the shower with water
because it feels like that is happening.

What does the magnetism between you and a lover feel like to you?

When you can't stop looking at each other and smiling, or
you want to kiss one another and hold hands.

What goes through your mind when this is happening?

What I am thinking is that I can't wait to get the guy in bed.

*Do you think it is possible to make women artificially feel that
magnetism?*

No, I watched "Don Juan," and I still don't believe it is
possible. Some men could do it who were really in tune with
their power and confidence. Women are really attracted to
powerful men. I don't think you can make up that feeling.
The only way you can do that is to empower the woman,
not by lying. When a guy is trying to force an outcome it
just doesn't work.

If men could just give up that the only thing they are trying
to get is sex, then they would be more open and free for
women to provide that, rather than having men work so hard
at it. When men work hard at it, they give women all the
power. If a man could go out with a woman without trying
to get what he wants, without trying to manipulate her, force

an outcome, or try to control the situation, it would be an amazing date.

What would be the fastest way to get you into bed tonight?

Be very self-assured in what you are up to and give me lots of compliments like, "You are gorgeous," not bullshit compliments. Really pay a lot of attention to me and just be a complete gentleman. Make me laugh and be romantic.

I am not one of those prudes. If sex is there, it's there and I am not going to wait around. If I like what I see, I go after it. I don't keep a guy at bay for weeks. My hormones are usually raging during the first week.

What is the common element in all your wonderful sexual experiences?

One commonality is that they take control of me. They are committed to me having a damn good time and their needs are put second. They get more pleasure out of really pleasing me. In turn, I am so turned on that I just want to please them as well.

I definitely like going down on a guy. I enjoy finding his most sensitive part, touching him all over and caressing him. I like to use my tongue and tease him. I love to drive a guy wild, lick his inner thighs and suck on his balls, and use my tongue to play with his penis. I love it. I love it when they just want to throw me down and tell me I'm a bad girl and just go for it.

Do you like to be tied up?

I've had guys tie me up before, and I loved it. I was dating a guy in San Francisco who introduced me to the S/M community. He took me to parties. My favorites were the puppy pile parties where everyone was half naked and just chewing and kissing one another, men and women alike.

I remember one party where there were five of us on one bed and one guy was on top of me. He held me down with his hands. He had an ice cube in his mouth and he was rubbing it all over my breasts and around my neck. Another guy was whipping me very softly. And there was a room full of people watching and touching me. I can't think of anything better.

What were you thinking when that was happening?

I was just really relishing all the attention. I was blown away. I especially enjoyed the women who were kissing me and caressing my legs. Part of my body was red hot from the whip and part of my body was red hot from the cold. It was an amazing sensation, it was great.

What would be the ideal sexual experience for you?

I like all different types of sex. I like it rough, fast, and unexpected and I like it slow with candles and the right music. I like being dominated. What I don't like is when it is always the same thing. It depends on my mood. If the guy will take my wrists and shove them down so I can't move and then pin my legs down, that gets me so excited. I love it when a guy teases me, like massaging every part of my body very lightly, then lightly touching my vagina. If he uses his tongue and darts in and out of my vagina, that drives me bananas.

What goes through your mind when you are being held down?

I love being showered with attention, and I love being controlled. What goes through my mind is that I want the guy and I must have him. I can't wait until he actually penetrates me. At that point I stop resisting. I love wrapping my legs around a guy and the sweat between our bodies. I couldn't even imagine playing coy "Ms. Resister" in bed, it is just so not me.

What characters are you when you role play?
I have only done it a few times, when I was the obedient sex slave. I just did whatever he told me to do. Role playing would definitely be fun. I would like to play with a doctor-nurse fantasy. I would like to pretend I was a Candy-Striper and the doctor would use a lot of his tools as foreplay. Stethoscopes are always so cold, he would rub it all over my body and his little thermometer would be all over me. He would use his tools and give me orders.

Another one would be for him to give me a medical exam. He would tell me to bend over and I would be wearing my high heels with my garters, my lace teddy and my Candy Striper outfit.

Every man and every woman has a different way in bed. The more you can sleep with somebody, the more you realize what their likes and dislikes are. You can actually create really great sex with somebody. It is not necessarily great the first time you are at bat, but I really think that anyone can have really great sex as long as they are open to communicating about it. Also, they need to be open to what turns their partner on.

Why wouldn't you be open to a relationship with a woman?
There is just something about a cock that makes me smile. A plastic one just doesn't cut it. There is something about the way men smell and their power and their seduction. Plus, I love to feel the muscles on their back. It is the whole power that men have that just gets me excited and makes me want to be with them. Women are great to cuddle with, but not so great to fuck.

Name: **Claudia**
Age: **32**
Occupation: **Opera student**
Relationship Status: **Has boyfriend**

What qualities do you look for in the men you date?
I like creativity on every level. I like men who take obvious sexual pleasure in their bodies. The way they dress expresses that, as does the way they wear their hair. I like men who are intelligent and know things about topics I know nothing about. I usually don't go for conventional men. It is not a generalized thing, because the men I am attracted to don't have much in common with each other.

I tend to date men who are either professionals or in the arts. I date men who are musicians, sometimes classical or even rock musicians, writers, sculptors and cooks. I don't regularly come into contact with doctors or truck drivers.

What do you do when men approach you in public places?
Guys don't approach me that much because I don't like to be approached. I put that out. I want to be the one in control of when I get attention.

What is your reaction to men who come and talk to you? Do you like that and will you talk to him, or will you pretty much blow him off immediately?
He will have to do something to get my attention.

Like what?
It's very hard to be specific. I am going to size him up and I am going to either like him or not. If I like something about him, I'll talk to him. I will talk with a guy if he seems attracted to me and is not afraid to let me see it, or if he can do it in an honest and open way. If they are trying to impress

me, or if it's not me that they are seeing but only a certain image that they want to haul off to their cave, then I'm not going to talk to them.

So you would consider going out with a guy you met in public?
Sure, I've gotten into trouble that way, too. I'm not afraid to take a risk. If I like someone I will give him my number. I've made lots of really good friends that way.

Do you feel flattered when a man approaches you?
If he's honest I feel very flattered; I will immediately get interested in him. It has to be spontaneous and honest.

How do men show you that they are intelligent?
I end up being attracted to men who are good conversationalists and actually take pleasure in language. They generally have a very good vocabulary and sense of humor.

Do you date men significantly older or younger than you?
The last serious relationship I was in was with a man 16 years older than I am. The man I am seeing now is 12 years younger.

So he is 20 and the other guy was 48? How has it been going with the young one?
Fabulous.

Was it his personality that attracted you, or was it his age?
It was just him. The fact that he was young just gave me the excuse to go after him. I am attracted to tight, young bodies. I intended to have a summer fling with him. It seemed like a safe thing for a fling, because how could this possibly last? It was just for fun, and then we fell in love.

What is your advice for men on dating?

I would tell men to be honest no matter what. If all they want is a one night stand, I would advise them not to pretend that they want something else. That is one thing that has worked really well with me. Some people have put their cards on the table right away and I appreciate that so much. I think men need to be in group situations and have women friends around for support.

At what point during a date do you know if you are going to make a sexual move?

It depends on the situation and it depends on what I want. I almost always know what I want. If I'm in the mood to go and pick somebody up, I will go and do that. If I'm not, it will take a lot of persuading. If I am interested, I will just go out and do it.

How often do you pick men up and have a one night stand?

I don't make a habit out of going out and picking people up. If I am not in a steady relationship, I know myself, and it isn't healthy for me to go too long without any sex. So I do what I need to do. Now I sound like a guy.

You sound like a snake who must feast occasionally on her prey. How often have you done that?

I am 32 years old and I think I've had about six or seven significant relationships. I've had sex with about 50 people.

Are you aggressive during sex?

No, I think it is very equal. I enjoy being aggressive during sex because I really enjoy men's bodies. It depends on the man. I like men who are responsive and verbal. If someone just lies there and doesn't say anything or tells me what he wants, then I have no idea if I am giving him pleasure or not. How can you tell if your partner likes it unless they say something? If you will tell me what to do, there is very little that I wouldn't do for you. I love being asked. Tell me what to do, it makes my job so much easier. I like to talk during sex. I give directions and express affection. I let them know what I like and don't like.

I don't like abuse. There are different types of power exchange. Anything that is like punishment I am not into at all. In sex, power goes back and forth. One person is more dominating and the other is more submissive. I like it when someone takes control of me and I like to control someone else. I am not into discipline. I haven't yet experimented with bondage.

For me it is all about trust and I don't want to override a lack of trust. If I am going to tie someone up I want them to really trust me, because if they are defending themselves against me, then it will take away from the pleasure anyway.

What is going through your mind when sex is great?
Wow! Total awareness of physical sensation and almost a hallucinogenic kind of thing. Not so much a visual hallucinatory experience, but a breaking down of physical boundaries. It is metaphysical. I feel totally free and rather happy, playful and child-like.

Is there a difference between your fantasy sex life and your real sex life?
Less difference now than before. Now when I masturbate I don't fantasize as much as I used to. It is now much more a form of self-worship. I'm a diva, I'm an opera singer; I have to worship myself.

I fantasize about things I don't actually want to do, like having sex with lots of people all at once. That can keep me busy for a while. I also fantasize about various forms of exhibitionism.

Have you had sex in public places?

Yes, I've had sex in public places. I've had sex outdoors quite a bit, where people could walk by and see, and they did. I remember having sex in a concert hall with a man after the audience left.

What is your advice for men who want to have one night stands?

If you show a genuine interest in a woman, that is the best way to get her interested in you. Men need to realize that there are plenty of women out there who just want to have a one night stand. That's another thing that drives me nuts about guys, they want to have a one night stand and that's fine with me, but then the next day they always treat you like you want to get married and be in some committed relationship. Men should just realize that there are women who want exactly the same thing they want. They will probably have a better time if they find them.

Are you disappointed if guys come in two minutes?

No, as long as they don't just roll over and go to bed. I don't always have to have an orgasm. I can have a wonderful sexual experience without having an orgasm. I hate it when guys feel they didn't do their job if I didn't come. That really annoys me.

Name: **Andrea**
Occupation: **Legal Secretary**
Age: **29**
Relationship Status: **Married three years**

What goes through your mind when you are on a romantic date?
The world just looks softer. It's more of a feeling than a thought. I get a little fluttering in my heart. I get all giggly. I think wonderful thoughts about the person I'm with and I want to please that person.

What do you like sexually?
I am in the process of exploring exactly what turns me on. I like the sensuality of control and BDSM. I also like not being responsible, it allows me to enjoy it more. I like being teased for a long time. I like being tied up and brought almost to the brink of orgasm and not being allowed to come, and having this done repeatedly until I am begging for it. This is done with my husband going down on me, with toys, with his fingers, whatever. When the release does come, it's just incredible.

When did you start to experiment with being tied up?
I've had fantasies about this from as far back as I can remember. Even the guy I lost my virginity to, we played around with this. I lost my virginity when I was 14. I asked him to tie me up. He was 16 and it was pretty simplistic. There are people who are into it and people who are not. The people who are into it are incredibly creative because they're as turned on by the power-play as I am.

I had a one night stand a few years ago that was incredible. The sex we had was mind-blowing, but it was just one night. I've been talking to my husband about it. He knows my fantasies and he's just starting to understand that a big part of what I like is the mental aspect of it. We just started playing and it's been a lot of fun.

How does your being a submissive and your husband being a dominant carry over into your day to day relationship?
I like someone who is strong enough to make decisions. Sometimes I like to have someone make decisions for me. Sometimes I just want someone to take care of me.

In terms of control, does your husband have the final say in most areas in your relationship?
This is actually a new element in our relationship. This is a fantasy of mine that he is doing for my benefit.

It's a fantasy to have somebody just dominate me and tell me what to do. The more I get rejected, the more I want what I can't have.

Sexually, it is one hell of a turn-on to be something that someone desires so fiercely. It is very flattering. It's very primal, you don't have to take any responsibility. There's no guilt. "I couldn't help it, I was tied down to the bed, what could I have possibly done about it?" You get to just lie there and enjoy it.

What is the mental aspect of it for you?
For instance, one of the rules is that I can't masturbate without permission. Now, it's not like I do it a lot, but since I can't, I think about it constantly and I'm horny all the time.

What are the other rules?
I have to be available to him sexually at all times. We discussed it and it was probably my idea. I like being objectified. I am sort of his sex slave. I'm here for his pleasure. Sometimes we have sex just for him and other times we play for hours and have these incredible orgasms. The times that I don't come just build up for the times that I do.

I used to say, "Oh honey, I'm so tired. It's been such a long day." Or he would be horny in the morning, and I would say, "Oh God, I have to get ready for work." We would spend 45 minutes arguing about it. I realized that if I just shut up and turn over, it would be better for everyone. So we came up with that rule and it works well.

Another rule is that I can't whine, "I'm tired." If I do, I get a spanking. Also, I can't directly disobey something that he directly tells me to do. We have limits. He is not going to tell me to do something that I am totally uncomfortable with. For instance, I like playing around on the computer, and our America Online bill is absolutely astronomical. So if he tells me he wants me off in 30 minutes, 31 minutes later I'd better be off the computer.

How do you get punished?
Once when I was on the computer, I lost track of time and I wasn't off the computer when my husband told me to be. It happened to be a dominant that I was talking to. So my husband told me to ask the guy I was chatting with what he would do if somebody made such an infraction. The guy suggested that I be tied down to the bed naked on my stomach, be paddled one swat on each cheek, then left alone in the dark, and then come back in and do it again four times.

There are not words to describe what happened. The swats were pretty hard, so by the third time I was sobbing gently. My husband went really easy on me the fourth time. I got pretty turned on by it, and so was he. We had fun after the fourth swat.

What were you thinking when you were lying there all tied up?
I was thinking that I was going to watch the time from then on. I was also thinking that my husband is serious about the

rules, and he really means what he says.

Was it a turn-on that you had no control?

Yes. There is something erotic about being tied up spread-eagle, naked. You are so vulnerable.

At first when we were playing games before we set the rules, the problem was that I trusted him too much and I knew he wouldn't do anything, and so it wasn't nearly as much fun. Now with these rules, we've managed to put an edge on it. I know that there are repercussions for things and it adds a bit of excitement.

What do you think about when you masturbate?

When I masturbate I create vivid scenarios. I imagine whole stories.

What kind of stories?

Sometimes I imagine I'm in a room in my house and someone breaks in the house and finds me, and then takes me forcefully. The guy rapes me.

What turns you on about being raped?

Just being so unbelievably sexy to some guy that he can't help himself, he just has to have me. Again, the lack of responsibility is a turn-on. That is just a total fantasy, it isn't something I would want to have happen.

In my fantasy the guy is fucking the shit out of me. He pins me down and I can't move or struggle.

Name: **Roberta**
Age: **35**
Occupation: **Co-owner of a tattoo and**
                                   body art studio
Relationship Status: **Lives with a boyfriend**

What are the qualities you look for in the men you date?
I like men who are sensitive and compassionate and aren't afraid to be spiritual; those are the most important qualities. Also, someone who can communicate. One of the problems men tend to have is they don't communicate with women. Women really need to be heard and to hear. Communication has to be there and the sex has got to be good.

Do guys hit on you a lot on the street or out in public?
All the time. It depends on how I look on any given day. I pride myself on having a number of personas and looks. I can downplay my looks. If I just don't want to be bothered, the glasses come on, I put my hair in a pony tail, and wear big baggy clothes. I use all those things to my advantage. If I dress up and go out, many men take an interest and start talking to me.

What is romantic to you?
Sometimes my boyfriend and I go for walks in the park in the sun. That is one of the places we spend time together and get away from the stresses of life. Sometimes we consider it romantic when we have taken off a whole day and a whole night just to be together and make love and take our time, which is something we rarely have the time to do. We will spend seven or eight hours making love and really taking the time. That is what I consider romantic. Throw in some hot wax and you have a party.

Are you and your partner monogamous?
No, we are each free to do what we want.

Has what you've looked for in a sex partner changed over the years?
I was introduced to power and control at an early age. When I was 22, I dated a man who was 42. He was into S/M and I was very curious. I was much more submissive back then. He was really into being violated, being anally penetrated and urinated on. At first, I thought it was very bizarre, but I found it very interesting, even back then. This guy's favorite thing was for me to piss in his mouth. I learned to drink lots of tea, so I would have lots to give him.

How does power and control play out in your sex life?
Power is very much an aphrodisiac for me. The consensual exchange of power is mutually empowering. Even if the person is giving up power and being pissed on, beaten or fist-fucked, it is still empowering because they have the final say and are willing to trust and relinquish control. Trust plays a big role here, and then by extension, there is love. If there is trust, then there is some basis for love and respect. Love can be defined as ultimate concern for the well-being of another.

I am almost always in control, even if I am in the submissive role. I can get turned on by role playing. For example, if I have someone dress up like my school professor and I am the naughty school girl and he gives me a spanking, that's a real turn on. I am always the one who initiates it. Whether I am tying someone up and playing the black widow spider and he is caught in my web, or whether I am the naughty school girl who is getting spanked; I am the one who is initiating the scene.

Do you get off on inflicting pain on guys?
I get off on their reactions more than the actual pain. I know what pain can do in terms of transporting the individual in

terms of ego loss and ecstasy and all that stuff. I don't really regard it as a pain thing. It isn't always about pain. Quite often it is about giving up power and control. Pain can be one manifestation of that. Other times, pain doesn't even play a role. Sometimes the worst thing you can do to somebody is to put them in very snug bondage and tickle their nose with a little hair and it drives them crazy. There are a lot of ways you can play with power that don't involve pain, but they all have to do with control.

Are there aspects of sex play that give you an emotional release?

Pain can give me an emotional release. For example, if I was playing with someone and I was submissive, they could give me a very intense flogging that would allow me to break down in tears and just let it all go. It is very uplifting for me. There is a lot of tenderness afterwards when they hold me.

Is sex spiritual for you?

I like to view it as the Tantricas did, as a sacred rite that was never designed to be used for procreation. In fact, the ancient Gnostics were into elaborate rituals that included every form of sexual debauchery, except that which would lead to procreation. They considered the flesh an abomination. They thought that the Creator God who created the world of life, death, reproduction and flesh, was an abomination. They lived their life to practice dying on a daily basis. They found that when they did ecstatic sexual rites like flogging, they could experience dying, meaning to surrender to God or "being-ness." So, sex became a spiritual potential. Other cultures went the other direction and went into celibacy.

Sexpectations

Chapter 2: Extreme Women

Chapter 2: Extreme Women

I t seemed so odd at first: to hear from a seemingly sweet and beautiful woman that in the hottest moments of sex she likes to be cut with a rug knife. How can it be? After hearing the extreme stories, it began to make sense. It even began to sound romantic and tender. When I could step outside of myself for a while and get into her perspective, I could see the tenderness, appreciation and consent between her and her partner. Who am I to judge what consenting adults do in private?

Extreme women are those who are living on the edge of sexuality. "Extreme" is not a moral judgment. It is a description of a lifestyle that constantly pushes the envelope. Most of these women have a rather normal life, but they have an edge that sets them apart. They take life to an extreme. They certainly push mainstream values and beliefs to an extreme. Importantly, they don't do this for show. Instead, it's just how they live their lives.

Sexually speaking, they are more intense, severe, extravagant, and radical than most women. They push the boundaries of what sexuality is, just as they push the limits of who they are.

This chapter features women who are into dominance and submission, handcuffs, pain, extreme bondage, bestiality, cutting, mistresses, and even religious zealots. Be prepared to be shocked.

Name: **Lilith Lovecraft**
Age: **19**
Occupation: **Fetish model**
Relationship status: **Single**

What qualities do you look for in the men you date?
I look for intelligence, someone who is very sexual, independent, extremely strong-willed, kind of androgynous, and someone who doesn't whine. I like guys who are obsessive and possessive about me. I find love/hate relationships to be very intense and I like intensity.

Where do you meet men you date?
I usually date friends of friends. I often meet guys on the street; they approach me all the time. I got hit on three times on the way home. Guys either think I am nothing special or they are obsessed with me.

Do you hear a lot of pickup lines?
No, I don't hear them that often. I have guys follow me around for a while and I usually have to start the conversation. At first glance, I don't look real nice.

Why don't you look nice? How do you dress?
I dress in between Gothic and punk. I wear combat boots, ripped up stuff, leather jacket and spiked collars. How I look often intimidates guys. I often talk to them after they give me the eye for a half an hour.

How does romance play out for you?
Once in a great while I can get very romantic, it depends on the guy. Most of my relationships have no romance. It is not a huge thing, but when I really care about somebody then it is really nice.

What turns you off in general?

Fat guys, bald guys, hairy guys; body hair really does me in.
A goatee is okay, but with a full beard you start looking like a
mountain man and it is pretty scary. I like young guys; I don't
like older guys. I like guys from ages 15 to 25. Generally
when guys are under 18, I don't mess with them because
they are illegal, but they look awfully nice.

Are you attracted to the bad boy image or the shy guy image?

How about the shy bad boy? I like guys who look harsh. My
ideal kind of guy has really long died black hair, white skin,
makeup and lots of black and leather. I like the anti-social
type who doesn't talk a lot. I go for the outcasts because they
tend to be smarter than other people.

*What clothes do you wear when you want to attract a lot of male
attention?*

I wear my thigh high leather boots, white leggings and
fishnets over that. And I have an ankle-length stretch velvet
dress that laces up from the navel to the chest and I leave it
mostly unlaced and it is slit down, kind of like a gladiator
skirt so it hangs down on the sides and back but shows your
legs. When I wear that, I have both men and women
following me around on their hands and knees willing to do
anything for me.

I go for the Gothic look. I go for that fetish thing because if
you just go for that dumb blond sexy thing, blond hair and
short skirt and all that, people are going to forget about you
later. But if you stick out like somebody's fetish, they will
remember you for a while. They will get that obsessive thing
going. If my ego is getting low I dress up and go out and
make people stare at me. I think most girls do it, but I do it
better.

What do guys wear that turns you on?

I seem to have this problem; I like men who dress like girls. Not cross-dressers, but guys who look the guy in Nine Inch Nails. Guys who wear fishnets and tight leather. I have a serious vinyl fetish. If a guy walked up to me wearing nothing but electrical tape and cellophane I would be happy as hell. I like gloves above the elbow. I have a serious fetish for dyed black hair and long hair on guys. I can't stand tennis shoes, they have to have boots that are calf high or higher.

What are some of your sexual fantasies?

The most recent one I had spawned off from a half awake-half sleeping state when my mind wandered into some weird shit. I was just lying there and the fantasy started. I am obsessed with the singer from the band Marilyn Manson. He is a creepy looking dude about 6'3" and only weighs about 130 pounds. He is hot. I have a fantasy about him where I am on top of him riding him and I have him tied up. I have one hand over his eyes and another hand over his mouth. I am riding him and as he starts coming I start choking him and he passes out. At the same time, I am screaming obscenities at him.

I am into that dominant thing. I would like to find someone who could dominate me, but I have yet to. I like to take the aggressive role more than the slave. I don't like the tie up and whip thing, because I think it's kind of fake.

Do you tie guys up?

Then they're not much good. I do it once in a while if I really want to torture somebody. I do it more often if I am mad at the guy. In my old relationship with the guy I was engaged to, it happened often. I would tie him up and tease him, now what is he going to do? I would tell him that I could do anything I wanted to him, then I would torture him mentally and physically.

Do you enjoy torturing men mentally and physically?
Yes, I get a definite kick out of it, but I hate being tied up. If they can pin me down and hold me there, that is really cool.

Do you have rape fantasies?
Yeah, I like a man to really rape me. It has to be somebody I know. With my ex, I would sit there and mess with him and tell him that I wanted other guys and all this. I am really abusive to men. I would sit there and torture him with all these ideas and I would start messing with him physically while I was doing this. Then he would finally hold me down and fuck the living hell out of me because he was pissed, but he was turned on at the same time. That's what I like, that's what I need.

How do you decide what fantasies you are going to act out and which ones to keep to yourself?
It depends on the guy. Some guys are really limited. Some guys are really soft and sensitive. There are many more sensitive guys than girls give credit for.

Don't you often find people to be wimpy about sex?
Yes, definitely. I tear the living hell out of half the guys.

Are you into pain?
I used to be into self-mutilation, but I would never let anyone else do it to get off.

Would you let a guy spank you?
No way, spanking is silly. If someone bent me over his knee, I would laugh my ass off. Once in a while I like a guy to hold me down on my stomach and bite the back of my neck while he is fucking me.

Is monogamy essential to you in a relationship?
Yes, I don't share.

Would you have sex with another woman if your boyfriend begged you?

Fuck no. I am totally straight. In general, I like to test other people's boundaries. I know what mine are, and I would never do another chick.

Do you worry about STDs or AIDS?

Every single guy I have been with has been dragged in and gotten a physical exam, an AIDS test, and a test for STDs. I make most guys wear condoms because I just don't trust them. I don't like condoms. I like to feel a guy ejaculate. There is something distinctively unsexy when I want a guy to come on me and they have to pull out and take a condom off to do it.

What do guys do when you are fucking them that really turns you off?

The worst is when they talk too much and they don't know what to say. Another turn-off is when a guy is dominating me and I am struggling, but I know I want it. Once in a while I say "Ouch" when something hurts and usually the dumb ass guy will apologize. I will say, "No, you idiot, you are supposed to hurt me," which breaks the momentum. I also don't like being called "baby," and that other mushy shit.

What is your mental state during sex?

Either that I am molesting this guy and he doesn't want me to, or that the guy can't resist me.

What is your advice to guys on how to please women? What do guys not know that would help them?

Every female is different. The world according to Lilith is, don't worry about the way she feels. If she doesn't have the guts to tell you what she wants, don't bother with it.

If I was a guy and I was with a girl and she wouldn't tell me what she wanted, I wouldn't bother with what she wanted. I would do what I wanted, and if she told me what she wanted it would be cool.

Tell me about your interest in S/M.

I am a model for a bondage fetish wear catalog on the internet and I've seen what that's all about and I've known people who are into it. I have always thought it was kind of silly to tie some guy up in lingerie and make him call me mistress. I think it is stupid. And half the whips they all have are really wimpy and don't even hurt, it is more the symbolism.

Do you find a sense of spirituality in sex?

Yes, it is more emotional than physical. There is no better way to get to a guy than through his dick. It's like "the best way to a man's heart is through his stomach," I've updated that.

I feel a strong connection with certain people, like I've met them before. When I meet some people I feel like they were friends with me when I was a kid, but I don't remember them. Those are the people I tend to be closest to. I can't really explain why that happens.

Do you manipulate men?

I like to play mind games, but at the same time I am really honest and never lie. I like to play mind games and see how people react. I like to know people's fetishes. I like to be in a guy's mind. I like to really have him in a state of lust. It isn't his heart, it's his mind. If a guy can't get you off of his mind he is yours.

What is your advice for men on sex and dating?

If I could give guys one word of advice, I would tell them to smell it before you lick it, know what you are getting into.

How many men have you been with?
Thirteen, lucky 13. I am considered a good girl.

What does it mean to be in the Gothic scene?
I like the whole vampire thing. I have cut guys with a carpet
knife and drank blood right from their skin. I don't let
anyone cut me though, but I could cut them all day long.

*What is one unusual thing that has happened while working at your
modeling job?*
I had one guy offer me $200 an hour to tie him up, burn
him with cigarettes and beat the shit out of him with a bat.
He was a guy who called my work and had seen me on my
web-page. No way would I do that. I might tie him up and
take his wallet and run away with it. That would be fun. I
might slap the guy a couple of times just for being so dumb. I
deal with a lot of weirdos. Lots of guys just want pictures of
my feet.

Name: **Julia**
Age: **31**
Occupation: **Computer Sales**
                             Lives in London, England
Relationship Status: **Single**

What qualities attract you to a man?
I look for intelligence, humor, and a very, very filthy mind.

Where do you usually meet the men you date?
Oh, all over. I meet them at work, at the library, at the shops, at night school, everywhere. Work is a good place to meet men, although you have to be careful.

What do you want men to know, and what do you want your partner to know about women and dating?
I want them to know everything about how to arouse me physically. They need to know how to take me slowly, and when to take a chance on the opposite. They must be able to read me. I don't need a guy to understand about periods, hormones, or anything like that, but he must know about language and how to use it in an exciting way. A guy who can say things the right way and varies his approach can have anything he wants.

How would you feel if a man came up to you, introduced himself, and asked you out on a date? Do you feel flattered?
No, I don't feel flattered. My initial feeling is always arousal, but I usually end up rejecting him even so. The arousal is because I think "I am this close to sex," but I will only go out with a guy who has the right sort of personality.

How do you let a man know you are interested in him? What signals do you give him?

Goodness, lots and lots of ways. I've used them all, some really corny ones, like licking my lips. I know it's really crude, and that's one reason it excites me so much to do it. Another is showing off my legs. My body language gives me away like this. I've even flashed my panties on occasion. Sometimes I say things with double meanings, but I have been quite blunt. There was a professor at summer school when I was doing Open University. I couldn't get his attention properly since he was being so professional, so I just said "If you want to, you can take me home tonight." Just like that. God, I felt like such a hussy saying that.

What turns you off in men you date?

Lots of things turn me off: arrogance, over-confidence, aggression, men who swear and deride their friends, religion, and possessiveness are a few.

Who usually makes the first move?

That depends on what you mean by "move." Like I said, I can be very suggestive, so a guy knows I'm available when I want to be. But he always makes the first move the first time. Once we are lovers, it's 50-50.

Do you find confidence attractive? Is confidence a requirement in men you date?

Yes, confidence is nice, but not vital. I've been out with guys who have none at all; that's quite nice, too.

Are you attracted to more the bad boy image, or the shy image?

I like shy boys because I can mold them to my own whims.

What was the most fun date you were on? What happened?

The most fun sexually? I couldn't pick the best. Here is a recent one: I had arranged to meet a guy from a client's firm one evening in my hotel bar. I was a long while getting dressed and ready, and when I got down I was ten minutes late.

I was pretty sure he had gone, so I accepted a drink from an older gentleman at the bar. He was in his 70's so I thought I was pretty safe, but he was very suggestive, and after I'd had a couple of gins he started to stroke my leg under my skirt. I was really aroused and responded a little by touching him on the thigh. After a while I suggested that we move to a more secluded table, and when we got there, there was no holding him back. He was all over me, kissing my neck and stroking me through my panties. I was very turned on and I had become quite forward myself, openly stroking his cock, when a face popped around the corner, and it was of course my friend from work. Well, he joined us and we ended up having the whole evening together, the three of us.

I never speak to my friend from work, but my elderly friend writes me every week, and I will see him again.

Is monogamy essential in dating situations?

No, I like it in my partner, but I can't stick to it myself, so I don't get too upset if a guy spends a night at his "cousin's house."

Would you ever have an affair or cheat on your husband or boyfriend?

Yes, very much so. I was married for two years and in that time I must have cheated on him 40 or 50 times. I had a long-running love affair that went on right through that time too, and still goes on today.

What was the shortest elapsed time between meeting a man and going to bed with him?

About three minutes. I've been to bed with lots of guys who have visited me at home as plumbers, milkmen, postmen, gas-man, and so on. I love that scene, tempting them, a nice long shag upstairs, then they go away back to their lives.

I used to sell cosmetics door-to-door, and slept with a few partners then as well. Why? I love the excitement. I'm addicted to the smell. If a guy plays it just right he can have me. I can usually tell within a few sentences if I like a guy or not.

What is the fastest way to get you into bed?

Any guy who reaches out and rubs my mouth with his fingers gently, or who pulls me close and bites my ear. Another thing that really turns me on is if a guy puts his hand on my knee and slips it under my skirt. I know these are not subtle advances. I suppose I get a kick out of their crudeness, but if it's done playfully or warmly I just start to get wet straight away.

Do women control sex?

Yes, we have the means of production. I know that 90 percent of men would sleep with me if I played my cards right. They have a 10 percent hit rate.

What are some of your sexual fantasies?

I have a million. I'll tell you just a few of them: tied to a bed and used by several guys; submissive slave to a master or even a mistress; turning my boyfriend into a sissy-girl; fucking a vicar, a policeman, or a judge on duty (I imagine sucking a judge off during the trial, me under his bench giving him head for an hour or so); me as a schoolgirl in a sort of grown-up's school; having a trained slave to tease and torment; golden showers; dogs, going to see the doctor and ending up in stirrups while he fingers me to orgasm; me as a real life servant to someone rich and powerful or a wealthy couple; eating two guys at once; being the only girl on a team of rugby players and having to satisfy them all; being fingered by a young female shop assistant while I try on clothes; and having a foot worshipper.

When did the kinky ones start? Well, most come from those dirty discussions we had as 14-year-olds at school. I just wanted to try everything.

What are some of your friends fantasies or kinky fantasies?

I have a friend who wants to lick a guy's poop off his bum! She is wicked, though, and she tells me sometimes how she's done it before and how turned on she was.

What are some sexual pet peeves, things you hate that men do or talk about during sex?

I hate it when a guy tells me he's coming. I always know already. I hate it when a guy tries to fuck my bum without any jelly. My bum doesn't lubricate on it's own, and guys need to know that. I hate it if a guy looks at his watch, or even wears one during sex. This only happened to me once, but I'll never forgive him.

Do you ever have sex in public places?

Yes, I've had sex in the cinema a lot, usually just playing, but also blow jobs. I love to go down on a guy in the cinema. I also made love on a park bench once during the day. I used to wear long wide hippie skirts so I could just sit on a guy's lap and he could take it from there. Do you count in cars? I've had so much fun in cars, but I've been caught a few times too.

My all-time favorite was at the opera with my boyfriend. I was wearing a really gorgeous outfit but kept my gloves and fur coat on since it was so cold. We touched each other a little and got quite horny, but the best part was in the third act he had a jacket on his lap and I got his cock out. The touch of my leather gloves sent him wild and he just went off straight away.

When he finished, I looked at him and put my scummy glove to my face. I'd spent an hour on my makeup, and I licked the cream from my fingers. He went berserk. His eyes nearly popped out of his head. Later on, when we were leaving, the old guy who had been sitting next to Pete (on the other side from me) gave me a wink as he walked next to me. I smiled back at him and when he held the door open for me, I walked through and then just stopped as he followed me through.

What lingerie do you wear when you are trying to please your partner?

I wear black stockings, garter belts, basques, half or quarter cup bras, and more.

What specific sexual acts turn you off?

I get turned off from tickling, a guy who wants me to kiss his feet, when a guy sucks on my nipples too hard, and of course enemas.

Do you use accessories when you are having sex?

Of course. A few of the items I love to use are whips, a crop, a paddle, blindfolds, gags, handcuffs, a dildo, and a vibrator. Some I haven't yet used but want to include carrots and candles, a rack, a school cane, and a dog collar.

Have you experimented with your fantasies?

Yes, to an extent. Sub/dom games have always gone well, although they don't happen often enough and not for a long time. I never suggest these things. I have long wanted to dress a lover up in my clothes, make a "woman" of him, and I read everywhere of guys wanting to do this, but I've made hints and only got close once. He looked so gorgeous I could have eaten him up, but he wanted to stop at the undies, and then take them off before I got "out of hand."

What is the "darkest" sexual act you've explored or acted out in your lifetime?

I've done lots of nasty things. A guy I was with once peed into a wine glass and made me drink it in front of (unknowing) friends. My breath stank so I followed it with a clove of garlic.

Another time, the same guy made me go to work with cheese in my knickers. I wore very thick tights over them but was still whiffy by the time I got off duty at twelve. When I got to his flat he pushed the cheese into my pussy then ate it out again. Sadly, we broke up soon after that when his wife got suspicious, but I always wanted to meet another guy like that.

Would you ever have sex for money?

I have done it twice. Once when my lover made me do it at King's Cross in London. I had to take the first punter that came along and do anything he wanted. He paid me ten pounds and wanked over my face. When I got back my lover fucked me so hard I was sore for a week! The other time I'm not telling about in this interview.

What makes a good lover for you?

A mind like a sewer.

What is ideal or good sex to you?

When I feel like a real slut. I hate feeling like I'm doing the "right way." I want to feel filthy and rude.

What is the most bizarre sexual experience you've had?

When I was tied up and had my pussy spread with butter, then I was licked out by a black Labrador.

Do you enjoy pornography?

I absolutely adore pornography. I love filthy stories, but get too turned on to finish writing one myself. I also like pictures of cocks coming, especially facials. Oh, and I love pictures of girls getting together with other girls.

Name: **Barbara**
Age: **32**
Occupation: **Works at an auto club**
Relationship Status: **Single**

What about S/M do you enjoy?
I like the sense of being controlled. I like a man to be in control of my reactions and I like it when he forces me to react in certain ways. I am not into humiliation, but I enjoy being spanked. I am more into sensation play, like depravation of sensation as punishment.

What would be an example of sensation play?
One example would be for a man to make me watch as he pleasure's himself, not allowing me to be touched. Also, making me beg and begging for touch himself.

Sensation can be done with blindfolds and visual depravation. I personally like to be blindfolded and see what I am not getting and desire what I can't have in that moment.

When you are being teased by a guy is it easy for you to be in the role of submissive?
Yes, I can easily get in a submissive head-space.

What is that head space like compared to how you are right now?
It is a completely different world. I am not assertive at all. I am very quiet and have a whole completely different set of thoughts that rush through my head.

When you are being dominated, do you consciously change the way you think? Do you ever just think what is happening is stupid and you want the guy to stop and leave you alone?
If I am thinking those thoughts, I'm not in a submissive head space, therefore, whoever I am playing with has not set me or

put me in that place. So, it is probably not a scene I should be involved in anyway. If a man is not making me feel submissive to him, or if he is pushing buttons that make me say, "What the hell is this, get off of me," then there is a larger problem and we shouldn't be together. When we are playing, and it is good, the scene takes on a life of it's own.

What is the most bizarre sexual thing you have experimented with?
I've been involved in scenes where I've been cut. I'm not really into blood play, but that's the way the scene went.

What did he cut you with?
A knife.

Where did he cut you?
He cut me on my butt and on my shoulder. That is not really my style of play. I was actually playing beyond my limitations. I knew it would happen when I went into it. I knew that the couple I was playing with were much heavier players than I was. They were also aware of that. However, I wanted to see what my edges were so I could set my limitations.

Could you have stopped the scene if it was too much for you?
Certainly, I just wanted to push myself and see how much I could really take.

Did you bleed a lot when he cut you?
I didn't bleed that much, it wasn't a deep cut.

Do you still have a scar?
No, it wasn't a deep cut. It was a surface cut. It was mostly because I like fear play and because I was caught up in everything else that was going on at the time. I didn't even realize that I was being cut, at least the first time. He basically just scared me by showing me the blood on the knife. It was such a minor cut that I didn't even feel it really. It was the visual impact of it that made a difference.

When I saw the knife with blood on it, it just made me feel even more submissive. He said to me, "Look at what I did to you. You gave me so much control that I cut you." It completely turned me on. It's a head-space you get into. I don't get as deep into it as some women I know. They can take a whole lot more pain than me. I always have a piece of myself that I hang onto which allows me to keep control over what is happening to me. I always retain the knowledge that I have a safe word if I need it.

What would happen if you completely let go?
I don't think I would ever let myself go like that. I don't know what would happen if I really did.

What do you mean by fear play, how do people scare you?
A lot of it is mental play. Domination is fear play in itself. You have to do whatever the person you are submitting to tells you to do or face the consequences. You can be punished through depravation of pleasure or threats of pain.

Within BDSM, pain is what is pleasurable for people it isn't punishment. So, threatening that if you are not good you will be spanked or hurt will only cause the person to be bad because they want the spanking.

A lot of people think anything BDSM related is this dark and terrible thing; I don't. But most people fail to see that it is consensual. Both people are being satisfied. Do you have any comments on this?
People into BDSM are more open and talk openly about their sexual practices. Communication is so much part of the whole thing. It is essential to know the other person's preferences, limits, desires and dislikes ahead of time. Most people I play with are completely comfortable expressing them and open-minded to other people's kink, even if it isn't our own kink. The key words are safe, sane and consensual.

Name:	**Alice**
Age:	**53**
Occupation:	**Medical and legal tran-scriptionist**
Relationship Status:	**Living with 36-year-old boyfriend**

How many submissive men have you had over the years?

I know exactly how many submissives I've had. I have a paddle that I bought when I was in Amish country. It said on it, "Board of correction," and I couldn't help but buy it. I have made every submissive sign it, and now there are 16 signatures on it. Some of them are regulars for the past three or four years, some were shorter term.

How did you get into D&S? Did a light switch just suddenly go off in your mind?

I have only been into it for the past five years, before that I was just totally "vanilla." I got into it after an intense sexual experience with my boyfriend. I began to read stories about D&S and became fascinated.

I get a rush from power and control. I was always just a quiet little girl who always said, "Yes sir." All of a sudden I was the boss, in complete control of my slaves. It has had great results in my life. I am much more self-assured. I am a better person for it.

What are some of your more unusual sessions?

My sessions are verbal and physical, but not sexual. There is no sexual contact with me, and there never has been.

One of the oddest sessions was the guy who never even saw me. He told me on the phone that he read in *Variations*, or one of those magazines, about a session with a man and a woman who talked on the phone and they decided to meet.

The woman told the man to go into her backyard, strip off his clothes and put on a blindfold that would be waiting on the back table. Then he was led into the house, where they had a session. In the end, she removed his mask and they fell in love and lived happily ever after. The guy I eventually saw told me he wanted that type of session.

I told him that I couldn't do it alone because I have never allowed a stranger into my home. I always meet them first and let my experience and intuition guide me as to whether I want something to happen. But I couldn't meet this guy ahead of time because it was contrary to his fantasy.

So, I planned this for a day when my boyfriend was off work. I told this guy to park in a remote parking lot in the middle of the afternoon, and to face the wall and not look in his rear view mirror, and I would come up from behind, blindfold him, and take him to my car. I can't believe I did this.

I came up from behind and handcuffed his hands behind his back, then I put him on the floor in the back of the car. I could have gotten arrested. I drove him to my house. My boyfriend was in his car behind us. I pulled into the garage and led him into the room I use as a dungeon. Then I uncuffed him, secured the blindfold and told him to get undressed.

At the end of the session he wanted to go to the bathroom and asked if he could take his blindfold off. I said that I would lead him to the bathroom and once inside, when the door is closed, he could take off the blindfold, go to the bathroom and replace the blindfold before he came out. Then I took him into the bathroom and handed him his clothes. He got dressed and I put him back in the car and drove him to the parking lot.

He said, "I'm not going to see you?" I said, "No." I told him that he could not turn around until he counted to ten and if he did I would tell everyone in the scene and his name wouldn't be worth anything. So he didn't see me. I got into my car and went home.

Do men have to make a commitment to be your submissive? What is your normal agreement?

They can have sex with their girlfriends, wives, and boyfriends. I don't care. But as long as they are making love with themselves, it is mine and they have to ask permission. Also, if you are mine you are mine and no one else's. I usually see my subs once a month. I don't want it to interfere with your business or your wife. I don't want to interfere in any way with your real life.

I want you to realize at all times that this is a game. This is not real. You are not really a slave. I can't sell you and I don't own you. We are doing things according to your list of no-nos. It is a game. People don't get hurt in games. I am not a dominant or a mistress unless I have a submissive. For me to tell you that I am a dom with no slaves is crazy. So I have to be good at what I do. I enjoy it and consider it my hobby.

What is a typical session like?

I like the basics, bondage and discipline. I whip them, stick nipple clamps on them, and do cock and ball torture, which is not as bad as it sounds. I don't believe in verbal abuse. Sometimes I humiliate them in public.

One time I took a guy shopping for panties, because I found out that he wanted to be forced to wear panties. I am not into feminization. I just want to be the means through which men fulfill their fantasies. If I don't respect a man I can't really play with him.

Most of my submissives are executives. One is a partner in a mega-law firm. I have another guy high up in NYNEX. You know who are submissive? Lawyers, oh my God, are they submissive! I have one guy who is an international banking lawyer and all he wants to do is give up and stop being "on." He just wants someone else telling him what to do for a while.

What is one of the most unusual sessions you have had?
I once had a double session that was the battle of the dominants. It was me, my male submissive, a male master, and his submissive female. The master told his slave that he wanted her to go down on my slave who was tied spread eagle standing in the middle of the room. His slave is on her hands and knees sucking my submissive. I looked at my slave and said, "You do not have my permission to come."

The master said that his submissive was going to win. I said that we had to put a time limit on it. This is not the kind of thing you can just say, "Let's see what happens." This submissive woman was working all she could. I ended up winning and the contest went on for a while. The master could not believe that he was so eager to please me that he would forego coming. My slave just wanted to please me. I told him that I would be very unhappy if he did. As a reward for holding out so long, I let him come. It was very fun, because I am very competitive and I won.

I once had a slave who drove five hours to see me. He wanted to clean my garage and the gutters, and then he decided on his own to clean up the twigs in the back yard. Then I told him to come into my dungeon. In response, he asked me if he did anything wrong, if everything was up to my satisfaction. I told him he did a wonderful job and then he said if he did everything wonderfully then there would be no reason to punish him. I let him go and he drove the five hours back home. He just wanted to serve a mistress. I saw him three more times and all he wanted to do was clean my backyard and the floors of my house.

Name:	Darlene
Age:	41
Occupation:	History professor
Relationship Status:	In committed relationship with 22 year old man

What is your advice for guys about dating?

Dinner and a movie is always good. If they are shy, what I recommend is taking the woman to a restaurant, but not a big fancy place, because they will have to sit for a long time with the woman and worry about what to say. Then take her to a movie, because you don't have to talk there, either. After the movie you have something to talk about, the movie. That is the recommendation I always give shy guys.

Personally, I always like spur of the moment things. Even if it is nine at night and he has a craving for ice cream and wants to know if I want to come with him. It doesn't always have to be a formal date type of thing. I love dates when it is laid back and relaxed and everyone can just be themselves.

What turns you on?

I've been getting more and more into bestiality. My standard phrase is to wait until a nice erotic moment when we are both turned on and comfortable and then bring up that I have desires that most people don't. Men usually say, "What is it?" I often say, "I can think of a lot of ways to play with Rover other than just playing fetch." I've never met a man who didn't get that right away. I've had varying responses from "It's not for me, but I don't care what you do," to "Can I watch? Can I watch? Can I watch?" to "You are degrading the whole human race and I don't want to ever see you again." It is better for me to know men's attitudes right up front rather then after I have a lot invested in the relationship.

Do you have sex with animals while you are having sex with your partner?
With my current partner, yes, I do. It can be very fun. It can be a solo activity or it can be a mutual activity.

What specifically do you do?
What do you do in real sex? What you can do in human-to-human sex can be done the same way with animals. Obviously, the dog has to be a male. I prefer dogs, but I have experimented with other animals. No way am I going to do it with a stallion.

You can basically do anything with a male dog that you can do with a human male. Of course I don't prefer female dogs, but I know men who do. It is just a different facet of sexual expression. I really enjoy oral sex and I really enjoy zoophilia. It's a spice, not my whole sex life. My partner is also a zoophiliac, so that works out well. We are both inclined in that way.

At some point you only fantasized about having sex with animals, and at another point you actually acted it out. There was obviously a bridge into reality. How did you decide to cross over and act it out?
It progressed over time. At first it was just a touch and then masturbating and things like that. And that was fun, so what can I try next? It has just progressed slowly like that. It wasn't like "O.K., I have this whole fantasy and I want to bring it into reality." It was very gradual. I started slow with exploration.

What was the first time like?
I spread milk on my nipples and had one of my cats lick it off. It was a thrill to have her laying on me licking while I touched myself.

What do you say to people who have a moral problem with bestiality?

I don't take people's moral insanity seriously. I am a dog lover; no pun intended. I am also an active animal advocate. I would never hurt an animal. In my experience, dogs especially, love it when I touch them. I consider my dogs my best friends. I see nothing wrong with what I do. If I did, I certainly would not be doing it.

How do you decide which fantasies to act out, and which to keep to yourself?

Some fantasies are meant to be acted out and some are meant to be held as fantasies. I have no desire to really act out my fantasies involving pain. I love to imagine being hurt, but in reality I know I don't. Real pain turns me off. If I am hurt; I can't be sexual.

What is it like being in a relationship with a man so much younger than you?

I love being with him. I have never found a man so sweet and open. I don't mind being his "teacher" sometimes. In fact, he was in a university course I was helping teach. It was the classic Mrs. Robinson situation, but it has grown into so much more. When we started dating he had only fantasized about bestiality, and now he knows more, and has tried more, than I have.

Given your age difference, and differences in life experience; is it really possible for you to be equals?

I don't really care. I am happy with him, and he is happy with me. I am definitely the one who has more power and control in the relationship, but that is fine with him. I like being a "mother figure" and girlfriend at the same time. I think this is the ultimate in romance, sex, ease, and friendship. This is the relationship I have been waiting for my whole life.

Name: **Kara**
Occupation: **Comedian**
Age: **38**
Relationship Status: **Single**

Are you currently in a relationship?
No, but I am considering being in one. I will marry into
another polygamous relationship. For religious reasons a man
may take more than one wife.

Is this part of the Mormon culture?
In my background I have been Mormon, but this time I am
marrying a born-again Christian. At least I am considering it.

How many wives does the man have?
I would be the second.

Is there a maximum number of wives a man can have?
No. In my last relationship, I was the sixth wife among nine.

How did the man pull that off?
When you have that many women, we all have our own
homes. All the women are self-sufficient. We basically all take
care of our own children and our own needs and he just
rotates where he is needed.

What are the advantages in being in a polygamous marriage?
For a woman it is great. First of all, you are not in a full-time
relationship so you have a lot more freedom to pursue your
own interests, and more freedom to be your own individual.
Also, when you do see him, it is more like the honeymoon
phase. You actually enjoy each other and when you are tired
of each other and start to bicker, it is a good time for him to
go and visit someone else. Quite frankly, I liked it because I
could call one of the other wives and say "He is getting on

my nerves, can you invite him over?"

Isn't polygamy illegal?

It is illegal, but that doesn't mean it is immoral. It is only in Western culture that polygamy has been majorly frowned upon. Most of the rest of the world in some shape or form has been performing this since the beginning of time. It was the Puritans in America that tried to stop it early on.

Does this mean that you can also take other lovers?

No, I am married to him for all time and eternity, and specifically only with him.

If you are lusting after another man and want to be with him, will you pursue it?

Not unless I break my wedding vows.

Would you ever break your wedding vows?

I have never had any reason to. I think it comes down to my religious beliefs. I made a commitment to God. I don't mind pissing off people on the planet, but I am not going to piss Him off. I was very satisfied in the relationship and all my needs were being met, so I didn't have any reason to look elsewhere.

Where do you meet men that you would consider marrying?

Because I would only consider seeing other polygamists, I meet them through associates or other friends who are part of the polygamy community.

How big of a community is it?

From what I understand there are 100,000 of us in Utah. We figured out that there have to be at least 8,000 men. We have a large community. One of the problems is that there are tons of little splinter groups. Though everyone may know each other, they don't all believe exactly the same way. Ironically, one of the groups that I haven't gone to is a polygamous singles dance that one group puts on. It is something of an underground community.

Do you get jealous of other women when you are in a relationship?
Occasionally that happens. What is common is that all the women bond together in a non-sexual way. I think women need to be close to each other anyway, and sisterhood is very easy. We are using a higher power anyway. We are following our religious beliefs. It really is just easier to have a sisterhood.

As you know, most people probably think that the men in this situation are making out like bandits. They get to have lots of women around them and have sex with many women, but the women don't have a similar opportunity.
The first question men ask me is if there are any orgies. And the first question women ask me is what night is mine. No, there are not any orgies, and Tuesday night was mine. There is a lot less sex that goes on. In my family, whoever was actually breeding got choice to be with the man. There were different times when each of us were breeding, and obviously, when you want to get pregnant you have to change the schedule. Other than that, we did have specific days set aside, but if something came up you could switch with another woman or whatever.

Was your husband having sex all the time?
That is what people think, but not necessarily. It is not uncommon for him to spend time with any or all of his wives and not have sex with any.

You are not interested in dating at all, only marriage?
I would date, but the man would definitely have to be looking toward a higher power. He would have to have

religious goals and be oriented toward God more than money.

What if you found the perfect guy, but he didn't want to be polygamous, he wanted to be monogamous. Would you still be with him?
That would be a hard one. But I have a feeling that the guy could be converted easily. Because there is no male out there that hasn't fantasized about having this type of life.

Does the man run the risk of going to jail?
Of course he does. That is why if you have two or three wives it is necessary to have separate living arrangements. Quite a few of the wives told their neighbors that he was a truck driver so there would be reason for him to be gone a lot. In Utah, they just turn their backs on it. Polygamists are usually tax paying people in the background who are quiet and make no noise, except for the few bizarre ones that like to go out on killing sprees.

Do the other wives have a say about another woman marrying the man?
Of course. When new wives are added, it is sanctioned by the wives that are already in the group.

What does that mean?
There is not exactly a ritual, but the women have to be okayed by the rest of us.

So if you hated a woman, she would not marry your man?
Right, she has to be accepted by everyone in the family.

Did you really love your husband?
No, I don't think I really fell in love with him for a couple of years. I didn't see it really differently from an arranged marriage. I saw my responsibility as a wife as just a job. What it really comes down to is just another job and another title.

Wouldn't you rather be married to a man you totally loved, and wanted to be around?

This is the 90s. Relationships that start like that last for about two years and then there is divorce, kids and lots of upset. It is a nice fairy tale, but I am not sure it is reality. So why spend your life pursuing something that may not exist?

Have you ever been with a man where it was a steamy romance?

No, it would be nice, but the chance of finding that one special person in this entire world is so slim. After you've been with a person for a while, they grow on you. You learn to love them.

If you were giving a man on the street advice on dating, what would you tell him?

I would tell him to not be so quick. That is one of the biggest complaints I hear from women. And yes, you can take that in a sexual way, too. I think men have a tendency to rush everything. Although men are very slow at commitment, where we think they should hurry up.

What else would you tell a guy?

The thing that is attractive above everything else is for a guy to stimulate my intelligence. If you can get my mind going, you can have the rest.

In your tradition, why does a guy want more and more wives? Is it better to have more?

Yes, more is better, so to speak. Different men have different reasons. The thing with the Mormons is to procreate and produce as many children as possible. Also, the people who produce a lot in this life will get richer rewards in the after-life. I heavily believe that, which is why I have five kids already. I need to have more kids because someone has to pick up the slack for all the single people out there.

Name:	Kathleen
Occupation:	Homemaker
Age:	35
Relationship Status:	Married

What would it take for you to have a one night stand?
I go by intuition a lot, and it usually works for me. Basically, I look at how the communication is going and if there is an interest, I pursue it.

If you a met a man you found attractive who was interesting, cute, and seemed normal and safe, would you have a one night stand with him?
I might. It's never happened. I've always been married or in relationships.

What if you were divorced, then what would it take to get you in bed?
At that point it probably wouldn't take much. I haven't been active for a long time. Giving me attention is really crucial. I would know quickly if the man was a good person or a bad person.

Is romance important to you? What is the ideal form of romance for you?
Basically the setting. I like candles and a dark room and music. And then, of course, touching.

Many people think romance and BDSM are polar opposites. Are they?
They're not at all opposite. It takes an awful lot of trust and love to get deeply involved in it. That's what a lot of people don't understand about it. They automatically think these people are only into pain and that's it. There is so much more that is a major part of it. Romance is a part of it. Yes, there

are definitely times when your master delves into romance.

What would be your ideal romantic situation?
Candlelight, dark music, and a dark room. Dark music being
like Nine Inch Nails or something.

*If a guy invited you over, and when you got there he had created a
whole world just for you, candles and Nine Inch Nails playing and
the whole mood set just for you, what would you think, and how
would you experience that situation?*
I almost go into another dimension in my mind. I shut down
life in general, all the stresses and pressures go away. My
concentration is just totally with him. This happens every
time I'm in a scene.

*What is the submissive trigger for you? What scenes make you feel
more submissive than usual?*
The romantic scenes make me submissive. I don't need any
triggers, it is instinctual for me. I've been submissive my
entire life.

Is monogamy essential to you?
I'm questioning monogamy right now. It used to be essential
to me.

Do you find power attractive?
Definitely. I find the power to control me very attractive. I'm
not talking about emotional power, but mostly of sexual.

Would you ever have an affair?
I've already had an affair and my husband beat me up for it.
So no, I wouldn't do it again.

Are you attracted to the bad boy image?
I always have been. I've had the nasty habit of getting involved with the bad type.

To what extent are they bad?
Many of the men I have dated have been involved in criminal behavior. My first boyfriend went to jail for breaking and entering. My husband is not the most honest person, either. Let's just say that there is a bad streak in him. Not extremely illegal behavior, he just dabbles in it. He's just a very selfish person.

What type of illegal activity is he involved in?
First of all, he has mental problems. He is on medication and is an alcoholic. Even before I married him he had a run-in with the law where he pretended he was Rambo. It's a really long story.

What does he do now that is illegal?
Just white collar crime. He shafts the company he is involved in. I don't know the specifics. His field of criminal activity has to do with stealing promotional items.

If you are with a guy and you are submissive to him, what is the ideal scenario for you?
His words and exactly what he says.

What would he say that would turn you on?
Just asserting his power over me sexually and the threat of punishment.

What would be a good punishment for you?
A whip would be good. I can take a lot of pain. I'm not into humiliation. BDSM is all sexual. To me if it's not sexual, it's power-tripping. That's great if people are into it, but it's not

my scene. The threat is more of a turn-on than the actual punishment.

Do you push the limits so you can be punished? Isn't that always the quandary with people who like pain, that punishment to them is not really punishment? Is deprivation of touch really the punishment?

Yes, I intentionally get into trouble. I just defy what the guy says to receive the punishment.

What goes through your mind when you are being tied up? How do you feel when you are totally helpless?

That is the total domination scene. If he is getting off on it, that intensifies everything. I get totally turned on in that situation. I'm in a different world. It's multi-orgasmic for me. The only time I can really orgasm is during a scene. It doesn't have to be intercourse. I can have an orgasm just from being tied up. I don't even have to be tied up; it can all be in mental form. That's how intense a scene is for me.

What is the most extreme sexual experience of your life?
The most intense thing I've ever done was being whipped until I passed out. This was just a few months ago.

Was that enjoyable for you?
It was great until I passed out.

What happened when you passed out?
All I remember was that I collapsed on the floor and I was out for a few minutes.

Did you pass out only from the pain?
It was definitely very painful. But I think the emotional feelings I had were so intense that I just passed out.

Why didn't you use a safe word?

I didn't want to. I seldom use one when I am in a scene. I won't get involved in a scene until there is already a lot of trust.

Name: Sue Ann
Occupation: Technical Advisor
Age: 53
Relationship Status: In a committed relationship

Where do you usually meet men?
Through personal ads and online services.

Have you met a lot of men in person that way?
Yes. I've met around 100. I live in San Francisco. I've met men here, and I've traveled to other areas to meet people, like San Diego, Chicago, Massachusetts, Texas and Seattle. I've met people from all sorts of places.

What qualities do you look for in the men you date?
I look for men who are comfortable with themselves, and who have practical fantasies about what it's like to be in a relationship. Some people are really impractical. I look for people who like themselves and are into a range of very solitary to very gregarious activities. What is important is that they are comfortable with themselves as they are, and that they like being with me. That makes a big difference when I am dating someone.

I'm a high-visibility member of the BDSM community in San Francisco. So for a lot of people who see me and watch me, it's a big deal to want to go out with me or to play with me.

Are you currently in a relationship?
I have a boyfriend now. I am basically a monogamous person. If we are talking about sex I am monogamous, though I date a lot. I may indulge in sexual behavior, but I do not indulge in fluid transmitting activities on an uncommitted basis. That

means I don't have intercourse with other people. I practice very, very safe sex.

What do you do when you are sexual with people other than your boyfriend?

The reason it is different talking to me compared with somebody who does what we call "vanilla" dating is that I play with other people. Usually, this play does not involve overt sexuality.

What specifically do you do?

We play with sensation which is really very stimulating. We might do what other people do on a date, like go out to dinner, talk for a while, and then decide to do a little power exchange.

What happens then?

I only play the submissive side of the role or power exchange, so the other person at some point will call the game on and will perhaps take hold of me. We will have already discussed ahead of time what is permitted and what is not permitted, where I can go and where I can't. They will know ahead of time that I will not have intercourse with them. They will know ahead of time that I will not do anything that involves fluid exchange. I only indulge in orgasm-producing activities with my boyfriend.

Many people view S/M play as not as polite and formal as you've described it. What is the difference between what you are discussing and the common public perception?

Long term players are polite and understand the rules. What I've found from all the ads I've done is that many people have read *Exit to Eden*, they've seen some bad videos, and they think that power exchange is all about people abusing each other, which it is not. What it's about is letting someone else control you. That may be as simple as being told that you will kneel upon entering the apartment. Or it may mean that at all times you will address your partner as "Sir," that you will retain a respectful attitude, that you will do as he requests without arguing.

What would a guy want you to do outside the sexual realm?

He might ask me to rub his feet. He might make me kneel, remove his shoes and socks and give him a foot rub.

Is that humiliation?

No, not at all. What is humiliating about giving someone a foot rub?

Nothing is inherently humiliating about it. But some people might say that being ordered to do something is humiliating.

It depends on how people are doing these things. I am listening in a way because I have been doing this for a while and the dynamic of most of the people I choose to play with is that they like service. They are very, very honored by the fact that I will do these things for them. The essence is not in what they ask me to do, rather it is in the fact that they ask me to do it. There may even be things they ask me to do that I don't think are so hot, and I do them anyway.

Like what?

I like to do things my way. I can be asked to do something and I can be told just exactly how it is to be done. As in, "I would like you to get me a glass of water. And I'd like you to walk over to the refrigerator and use your right hand to open the door, your left hand to get the water container out. I want you to fill the glass to a certain level, put everything back that is not being used, close the doors, and then bring that water to me on your knees."

What if you don't want to do it?

Why wouldn't I?

I know my moods change and fluctuate. Sometimes I am willing to do what people ask and other times I'm not.

That is the whole point of this. We've already agreed that I am going to give up the control for a set amount of time. It's not for a lifetime.

What if it is something that you don't want to do?

I do it anyway. That makes it hot, it's the whole idea. I am not submissive in my outside life. I spent 15 years in law enforcement. I was one of the first women police officers on the street, driving a patrol car by myself. I don't take a lot of anything from anybody that I don't feel like taking. I raised four kids by myself. I survived alcoholism and drug addiction, and I've been sober for almost 18 years now. I've done a lot of stuff for myself.

Playing the power exchange games are really hot for me because it is a place where I can let go. It's kind of like another drug. It's a really strange feeling. It's kind of like hang gliding, but you don't have to jump off a cliff. It's about letting someone else have that control.

What goes through your mind when a man is dominating you?

I get wet. It's hot, because I can feel the energy between me and the person and I can really let go. When I let go, it's kind of like jumping off a cliff.

In a typical situation, how much of it is doing things like getting his water, etc., and how much of it is more sexual?

There might be normal conversations during an evening. Most of the time we stick to the subject at hand, which is me serving him, or him telling me what he wants next. With my partner, we often start with me giving him a full body massage and work on from there.

At a certain point he will put me on my knees and stroke me from the head down my arms, getting me relaxed, giving me instructions on how to breathe. He will tell me to breath through the nose and out the mouth, and to quiet myself while he prepares the room for the play we are going to do.

Is it playing for you, are you pretending, or are you in a character?
I am in another place. I guess you could call it a character. It's kind of like going on vacation. I don't have to make the decisions. It's taking the attitude of service. I ask myself, "How I can best please him here?"

When I was still doing vanilla ads, one of the ads that I wrote said, "Seeking single male to indulge in a mutual spoiling contest." I got very nice results from that because that's basically what I see going on here. It is a win–win situation. With most of the people I have played with, each of us goes in there looking at how we can please the other person, not what we can get out of it. It's the pleasing them that is the turn-on for me. I did a lot of vanilla dating previously and it was very boring, pretty unsatisfying.

I remember climbing into bed with guys in the 60's and 70's and hoping that they would be good: "Does he know where the stuff is, and can he use it when he finds it?" I don't find that here because I am coming into it looking for what I can do for my partner, and that changes the dynamic.

Whether it is BDSM, making love, going out on a date, or whatever; I look to see what I can put into it that will please him.

What is romantic to you?
Being with someone who is sensitive to my needs and does little things to make me feel appreciated and loved. Whenever

I go to my current partner's place, he has fresh flowers on the table. The place is always made up as if he is expecting the finest company. He is very sensitive to what I need on a given day. And it is okay to say no to something he wants. In other words, I can say no and he won't have a fit. We hold hands almost everywhere we go. He strokes me on a very regular basis, he just reaches out and touches. He remembers things from one time to the next that are important to me.

What aspect of your relationship is hardest for other people to understand?

Some people have a difficult time believing that our relationship is very romantic for both of us. They equate dominance with humiliation and abusive treatment. The difference between abusive and dignified is in how my partner receives some of this. He would never do anything to me, or have me do anything that would make others look down on me.

In what circumstances would you feel humiliated and embarrassed, and in what circumstances would you not?

It boils down this way. If I go to an orientation meeting of the Society of Janus, where people are seeing if they want to join us, I keep my clothes on. I don't do things that are edgy. If we go to a meeting where everyone is a member or if all the guests have been warned ahead of time that this is a place where people do BDSM, then, if my partner were to ask me to not sit on a chair, but at his feet, I would do it. It would be hot, it would be fun.

Talk about your journey between fantasizing about being submissive and into S/M, and actually living it out in reality.

First of all, I didn't have fantasies about it. What happened was, someone pulled my hair just right in March of 1993. And for six months, he and I did each other. He was also submissive.

We were kissing and he pulled my hair and then he nuzzled into my neck just right in that really sensitive spot. And my reaction to that was to be very aroused. So he did it again and I did it again. I would have fallen on the floor if he hadn't had a good grip on me. It was electric.

So you were a total vanilla girl before that?

Yes. The guy I was with said, "What do you know about dominance and submission?" I said, "Like in the dictionary?" And he said, "Oh my dear, we have to talk." He led me by the hand into his living room and sat me down on his couch. It was the classic knees touching and holding position, and he poured out all the things he liked to do. I had known this guy for close to 25 years, but we had just gotten personally involved in the last month. Instead of being turned off by what he was telling me, I was fascinated. He talked to me about the things he liked to do and talked me into trying some of them out.

He is one of these people who is really non-threatening, and it was really easy to go along with him. He is a very personable person, very smooth, and very soft, not aggressive in any manner. After six months I needed more than we could get out of each other, so I launched an ad for a master and joined the Society of Janus.

What did you experiment with?

We took turns tying each other up. I'd tie him up and spank him or do things to him that he wanted done. He liked being verbally abused and I didn't, so we worked that out. He tried verbally abusing me one time, but I got the giggles so bad he realized it was really going down the wrong road.

What kind of talk do you like to do?

I like being told something is going to happen and there is nothing I can do to stop it. "It is coming and don't you wish you could move, but you can't because I've tied you down." I like the idea that there is something being done to me that I can't get away from, and my partner wants to do to me.

I like being subjected to someone else's power. Again, this goes back to my desire to play with people who are really powerful. I like the bad boys, the motorcycle riders, the judo players, the jocks, the people who are more likely to want to take you by the hair than the hand. I just find people who are a little more polite in doing it now.

Do you get turned on by verbal abuse?

One of the first people I met when I did the ad searching for a master, said that a submissive or a slave is like a very old and valuable violin. A slave needs to be guarded, cared for, polished, waxed, and the strings should be kept in good order. In fact, those strings needed to be stretched in order to produce the highest and sweetest music. If somebody wants to throw the violin on the floor, or acts as the gift of my submission is less than wonderful, then I shut down immediately. I am very sensitive to the fact that I like being desired. I like pleasing my partner. So, to me, verbal abuse suggests dissatisfaction with my performance or with me, and that turns off the dynamic.

But doesn't verbal abuse at some level go hand in hand with the theme of you (the slave) having no control over what happens to you? The dominant can do anything they want to you, including calling you any name they want. You are their slut if that is what they want to call you.

"Slut" is a term of endearment in the S/M community. It just means someone who rarely gets enough of whatever it is. "Bitch" is a negative word, and it comes across that way. It is very negative and has no sweet connotation or double meaning to it. If someone were to call me a piece of shit, "bitch" and "shit" are just the same.

I would say that this is peculiar to me, but it's not. I've found this to be very common. Some women like verbal abuse, but most of us who play do not. That's why I see most of the people as fairly healthy. I don't need to be made to feel like nothing. There is no part of my psyche that needs to feel less than another person. Verbal abuse, by the way, is something that many men like to do and many of the submissive men like to receive. It is very popular for men, but very few women enjoy verbal abuse.

Lots of women have rape fantasies. In their fantasies they are taken against their will. A rapist obviously would be very abusive, both verbally and physically.

But rape fantasies are not about being raped, but losing control. When people talk about rape fantasies, it is an opportunity to enjoy total loss of control, being totally overpowered, but it is has to be safe. It has to be with someone they know is not going to cross the line, someone who really does love them under all this stuff. Or someone who loves what they are doing for them. For people who enjoy a little bit of humiliation or a lot of it, then the rape scene would probably include this. I find that most women who have had rape fantasies, and I am only talking about a very narrow sample here, are people who like some form of verbal abuse.

One of the things I like about people in the S/M community is that we talk about what we will do if something goes wrong. We have a "plan B." I don't think that happens in a lot of other places. Most people don't talk about what is going to happen, they have this idea that they will just be spontaneous. That is a good way to get into deep shit. I don't want to say "No" in the middle of a really enjoyable evening, so I need to let you know where I cannot go or where I will not go ahead of time, which means we've got to talk about it.

Most men are not used to talking with women about this. The ones I've talked to outside of the BDSM community need permission to dig around and talk about it, until they can get out exactly what it is that they want to ask or say. At least twenty to thirty of the hundred men I've played with, when I ask them why they are answering an ad from a woman in my age bracket, and they are in their 40's or 50's, say that the women they've met between the ages of 28 and 45 are nuts. They have a rigid idea of what you are supposed to do and how you are supposed to do it, and often what you are supposed to look like. And if you violate this list they are carrying around, then you are out.

If you want to do something, ask. We are in an era when a man doesn't know if he should hold the door open or not. He doesn't know if he should pay for dinner or not. Should he offer to go Dutch, or what? These things should be done ahead of time. Men at this point are dreadfully confused, but women assume that men know exactly what they should be doing. The fact is, everyone is confused. Talking works really well.

I have a friend who is a flight attendant, and he is a man. He said that when most of the women he works with talk about men, it would make your blood run cold. There is no way for a man to qualify with their criteria. These are women of a fairly wide age range, from their late 20's up into their late 40's. It is difficult for a man to know what a woman wants. The only thing I can see is for a man to open up the topic of talking about things, asking her what she believes in various areas. This may mean making up a list of questions ahead of time.

What are some of the best lessons you have learned through your participation in BDSM?

One thing I've learned from one of my partners in S/M is to ask questions. At the end of playing, all of my partners would always thank me for playing and one of the guys said to me, "I've really had a good time. But I want to ask you something. What could I have I done to make this better?" I could have fallen over. I wish I'd learned that 20 years ago. This guy could have asked for anything after that. My opinion of him went up 300 percent. I had never had a man ask me that before. I've had men ask me what I like. It was incredible. I have incorporated that into my life. It allows growth, it isn't criticism. I was much more used to someone criticizing my performance. Most of the time the answer is that everything was fine.

My best days are when I get up and ask what I can do of service today. It takes out all the power struggles. It allows me to be a positive note in life. This doesn't mean that I let people walk all over me. I let go of my need to win. You really don't have to struggle. You really don't have to indulge in a battle all day. When people date, they get into the same battles about who is going to win. If they would sit down and talk about what they need, and maybe divide up their charge of different situations, it would help them get along better. It works well and gives you the time to do the things you love to do together. If I really like someone, it doesn't make sense to be fighting with him all the time.

Sexpectations

Chapter 3: Romance and Dating

Sexpectations

Chapter 3: Romance and Dating

Romance and dating go together. What do we look for in a date? Is it the excitement of making an instant connection, the playful combination of language and expression, or the feeling of lust building by the moment? Or is it all of these?

When I set out to create this book, I hoped to find some answers many men have about dating: Where can I meet women? What is the best way to approach them? What do they want out of a date? Of course, I didn't find a single sure-fire formula. I got indirect suggestions, half-truths, opinions, and contradictory theories. It made dating even more confusing.

Romance is even more difficult to describe and quantify. What is underneath the traditional notions of flowers, candy, and candlelight dinners? Why do these things make a woman's heart sing so beautifully? What else has the same effect?

There is no short answer to the puzzle of dating and romance, but several trends became clear as I interviewed women. I am pleased to pass along their suggestions about what men should do, and what they shouldn't do. After dozens of attempts, I can personally vouch for many of their suggestions.

Confidence

Nine out of ten women mentioned confidence as *the* key quality that attracts them to a man. This is not limited to the way that men talk to women, but extends to men's confidence in their own lives. Older men, for example, were frequently mentioned as having the inner strength to talk to any woman, any time. "Nice guys" might get women to talk with them and be friends, but in the end they won't get them into bed.

Confidence can take many forms. A confident man knows who he is, acts without hesitation, and carries himself accordingly. He speaks his mind, keeps his word, and is willing to pay the price of being accountable. Women also perceive a man as confident when he has a stable career, or he is driven to further his career. Drive is displayed by focus, concentration, determination, and a need to better himself.

Romance

The women I interviewed identified being romantic as essential for men. Romance is not a specific action, but the thought behind the action. More than giving material possessions, it is a quality of being attentive. Romance can be perceived as appreciation. Giving a woman flowers warms her heart because it is a token of your affection.

For women, an essential quality of romance is the feeling of being comfortable and safe. This is often a function of having an open heart, being funny, and displaying thoughtfulness.

Miscellaneous Advice For Men

- Be present with her. Make your interactions with her personal, not generic. Don't try to bullshit her. Give up controlling the situation. Pay attention to her, and truly listen.
- Sincerity is essential. If you lie, she will know it.
- Don't take sex and dating too seriously. Free yourself up. Have fun.
- When you are on a date, don't be a Doubting Thomas. Focus on what IS working.
- There is a paradox of being attracted to a woman and showing her you are interested, while not being too

forward or overly sexual.

- More times than I can count, women mentioned bad hygiene as a turn-off. Most women had been approached by men who dressed badly and smelled worse. Without exception, every woman found this to be a turn-off.
- Another common turn-off for women is when men seem desperate. As one woman put it, "I don't want some wimpy needy boy who is looking for his mommy." It is confusing. Men need to be strong and sensitive, but not desperate.
- Many women commented that they enjoy being pursued. They like the courting process. They like the excitement that goes along with open flirting. Men, ignore everything you have heard to the contrary!
- Be yourself. Do what you do. Find your own path. Be sexual and date in ways you feel comfortable. Always act as if you are the man you have always wanted to be.
- Lots of guys don't know when a woman is giving them signals that they are interested. The variety of signals is endless, but here are a few: eye contact, smiling, giggles, open body language, joking, touching, and glassy-eyed gazes.
- Many women suggested that men need to listen to them more. Listening is an expression of caring. It is the most direct access to intimacy.
- To meet women, do the things you would normally do if you weren't trying to meet a woman. Find a woman with similar interests, so you stand on mutual ground. Join a book group, go to the gym, attend rock concerts, and frequent coffee shops. Go any place that truly interests you, and the women will follow.
- On the date, take her outside of her normal realm. Go someplace special.

Name:	**Kelly**
Age:	**41**
Occupation:	**Waitress**
Relationship Status:	**Living with boyfriend**

What are some pickup lines that work well with you?
I don't think lines work that well. What works is rapport, and eye contact is really critical. Somebody who isn't afraid to look at me while he talks to me is important. It's a good sign that a guy is attracted to me.

What do you find attractive?
Self-confidence is really important to me, more important than appearance. Another thing that is attractive is someone who is attracted to me and shows it.

How does he show it?
By paying attention to me and flirting with me. Also, when they act like they are really interested in me and they want to get to know me. I notice when their pupils dilate a little bit when they look at me. The guy also has to have a heart, a big heart. And he can't be a pathetic whiner. That is the biggest turn-off.

Does showing heart make you trust the guy because you think he is a good guy, or do find it sexy, like you want to sleep with him because he is so sweet?
It is a definite turn-on. For me another turn-on is someone who is psychologically perceptive and fun, but not like a comedian. Also, someone who is a risk-taker and takes risks in conversation with me, like he might reveal some personal thing about himself. I like them to reveal personal information to me. Fun is also really sexy.

What is the shortest elapsed time you have had between your meeting a guy and sleeping with him?

I'm not really a fast girl. I'm sure it is a matter of at least days and even weeks. To me, some of the best part of lovemaking is the anticipation and the building of sexual tension and chemistry in the relationship. Even if I am really attracted to a guy, I will never sleep with him on the first or second date on general principle, because it would take away some of the fun for me.

On a typical first date, what do you do with a guy?
I would make out passionately. I probably wouldn't remove any clothes.

So the easiest way to get you into bed is to know you over time, be really flirtatious, and go slowly? To have sex with you, a guy would have to wait three or four dates.

Yes, and you have to move at my pace and establish rapport with me. I have to feel like I am not just a benchmark, that there really is something about me in particular that really turns you on.

Do you want a guy with lots of money to shower you with gifts and prove his love to you?

I am not that attracted to guys with money. If they have it, great, but it isn't necessary. I am much happier if a guy displays his affection through touching me and wanting me.

I read a book recently that described a theory from Neuro-Linguistic programming (NLP), about how people have different strategies of how they feel loved. Visual people want a lot of gifts and want to be shown that they are loved and taken lots of places. A more kinesthetic person wants touch, and auditory people want to hear their partners compliment them and sweet talk them.

*What advice do you have for men on what to say to women, and
how can they start a conversation that leads to sex?*

Attitude is really important, but it's hard to define. I think
women want to be appreciated. It is important for a man to
act like he is genuinely attracted to a woman. It shouldn't
seem like he is only trying to score or objectifying her. If you
are, she is likely to pick up on it. I think you can just be
genuine. It's a paradox, because you are trying to pick her up,
but not in some jaded or cynical way.

You don't have to say anything profound or amazing. You can
just begin a conversation about some ordinary thing that is
going on, like the decor of a restaurant, or whatever. It
doesn't have to be that profound; that is a mistake many men
make. You can even ask some open-ended question.

What would a guy do that would turn you on?

Before I answer that, I'm going to share a little piece of
advice with your readers. This goes back to self-confidence,
and I call this the "piece on the side" theory. One way to
have a lot of confidence and to feel attractive is to know that
there is someone in your life that likes you enough to fuck
you. You don't necessarily have to be in love with them or be
in a relationship with them. This can just be a friend, or
someone who likes you but you aren't madly in love with.
Once you have this person in place, it takes the edge off. You
don't have that desperate sense when you go out to meet a
woman. It is a good way to keep yourself confident and to
confirm your attractiveness and desirability.

In a nutshell, go out and fuck whomever you can get your
hands on. It's recreational sex and it will help your attitude.

The other thing that is a trap is the myth of serial monogamy,
or the feeling that you can only pursue one person at a time
and you immediately stop seeing everyone else. Not
everyone does this, but most people do.

I was talking to a guy today who had just started dating a woman, and his mistake was that he stopped seeing all other women and only focused on her. In the end she dated someone else. He clearly should have kept his options open. He was dating only one woman and he should have had a few options.

But we are focusing on how a guy can score. What is it going to take for a man have sex?

I don't think there is a formula. Almost everyone likes surprises. Someone who takes me outside my ordinary realm of existence is definitely exciting. If you can do that, you have an edge over someone else. In my life, the only time I had a one night stand, the guy didn't take me anywhere.

Does bullshitting and smooth talk work with dumb women?

Often, when a guy thinks he is bullshiting a woman, one of two things happens: either she is a victim and she falls for it, or she is playing the biggest game on him. He might get laid, but he may also get just totally fucked with emotionally, financially and in other ways. There are a lot of very dangerous and manipulative women out there.

What are the common turn-offs and mistakes that men make?

The biggest turn-off is a pathetic whiner. I have several examples. Most men know what I am talking about. Men need a level of confidence to bag a woman, so insincerity is a turn-off. Women are used to that and they screen for insincerity. Because men have such a strong sex drive, and women feel like they are constantly getting hit on, they screen for insincerity.

What other advice do you have for men who want to have one night stands?

One thing is not to be ashamed of wanting to get laid, not

being ashamed of your sexual desires. Being really honest with yourself is important. You don't have to be totally honest with a woman, but be honest with yourself about the fact that you want a sexual relationship.

A lot of men seem to have shame about that desire and they fuck with themselves and women. These guys try to act asexual when they are really feeling horny, and when it really comes out it seems unexpected. A woman will be angry if you give her mixed messages. So the answer is to be a flirt, be appreciative of her beauty and sexuality. Focus on what you want from her. Have some balls, don't act like some asexual father figure or some feminist guy from the very beginning.

Name:	**Megan**
Age:	**19**
Occupation:	**Caregiver for elderly**
Relationship Status:	**Has a boyfriend**

Is confidence important to you?

I like a guy who is confident in himself, yet tender. I like someone who is willing to open up to me and cry and say, "I need you here." Yet, I like a guy who can hold me tight throughout the night when I am having a bad night. Or a guy I can wake up at 3:00 a.m. and tell him about a nightmare I've had.

Is the "bad boy" image a turn on for you?

I've been through that phase. However, I make sure they have a wild side. I've never dated a guy who didn't have a leather jacket and a bike. Also, at one point or another, all the guys I've dated have been in the military. I've dated a lot of guys, starting when I was 12.

What about shy guys?

Shy guys are interesting, but they don't know what they want most of the time. Shy guys come up to me and don't say anything. It is not until they have had at least three beers that they will even talk to me. Once you get them talking they are fascinating, but guys who are more open and more aggressive are more attractive. The first thing my current boyfriend said to me was, "Your eyes are beautiful," and he didn't look down at my breasts or anything.

Do you like to be romanced?

I love romance.

What would be the ultimate romance to you?

The ultimate would be to have a man sweep me into his

arms on the spur of the moment just because he wants to. He would pick flowers for me on the street and say, "Because I love you, because you are my darling."

Ultimate romance would be in a rose garden having a picnic with soft violin music, Enya, or Nine Inch Nails. I would want him to talk to me as we lay on a blanket. Romance is to kiss and hold each other under the stars with a bottle of red wine and pieces of fruit, feeding each other. I love to play like kids and yet be lovers. That to me is very romantic.

What advice would you give a guy who just wanted to have a one night stand?

I would tell him to go up to a woman and say, "I don't want a relationship with you, but I find you extremely attractive. I'd really like to go home with you and pleasure you for one night. I would like to lick you and taste you and fuck you, and enjoy your body and to have you enjoy mine."

Do you really think that would work?

Yes.

That would work with you?

Yes, I've used that line and I've had guys use that line. I've had my boyfriend use that line on other women.

What is such a turn-off for you during sex that you need to get away from a guy?

When they don't listen to me. When I say no it means no. One time a guy did not listen when I said no. To me that is wrong, so I drew a knife on him.

What did you do with the knife?

I put it through his thigh, then I got up and left. He was bandaged up by some friends. It wasn't that bad, it was just a flesh wound. The wound didn't need stitches or anything like that.

Do you enjoy pain?
Yes, I do, I like to be tied up and whipped.

Do you enjoy other forms of pain?
I like to have cuttings done. I usually use a lancet. It is like a straight-edged razor blade, but it's for medical use so it's been sterilized. It's like a paper cut with a pattern. It just scratches you and then you bleed and have a scar.

Do you have scars all over your body?
I have some, but I take really good care of my body and make sure I heal well. I don't get scars where people can see them. I have a tattoo on my back.

What would be your ultimate lover?
My ultimate lover is someone who can pick me up and slam me against the wall and fuck me. He is also someone who will eat me out until I scream or fuck me in the ass. The ultimate lover is very forceful, and gentle and caring at other times. He will tease me, kiss me and hold me. He doesn't have to have a huge dick, he just has to know how to use it.

Name:	**Lisa**
Age:	**27**
Occupation:	**Programmer**
Relationship Status:	**Single**

How do you feel when men approach you?
It depends on how they approach me. If they are nice and pleasant and considerate, then I'm flattered.

If a man approached you and you were interested in him, would you give him your phone number?
I definitely would not give him my home phone number. I live in New York, give me a break. I'd either take his phone number or give a work phone number and work it like that. I don't give out my phone number because you just can't do that where I live. If I felt really comfortable with the guy, I might give him my work phone number.

What would a guy say that would impress you?
He'd obviously have to say more than a line. I would need to have a nice conversation with the guy and want to get to know him. If he approached me and started talking to me, he could talk about himself. I'd rather he didn't talk about me.

I realize that part of what will get me every time is if someone will pay attention to me. Pay attention to me and look me in the eye when you talk to me, those are the major things. If he seemed normal, I would consider going out with him. If I was attracted to him, sex is always part of it.

When you are dating a guy do feel like you control sex?
Now I do. The first couple of times I didn't, but I will never do that again.

How do you control sex?

I control the speed it happens and whether or not he is going to get that part of me. In general, I think women definitely control sex because there is so much of a taboo at this point on rape and date rape. Guys are watching their step so carefully that I think women have the control now.

How are you manipulative?

I'm not so much manipulative with men in general, it's more specific people. I can arch my eyebrow in just the right way to get them to feel bad enough and do whatever I want them to do.

Do you ever make the first move?

Yes, I am notorious for it. I start kissing a guy, or I might just grab a guy. Once, I wrestled a guy to the floor because I wanted this guy so badly and I was getting nowhere with the subtle signals. I finally just pinned him down and kissed him. Sometimes you just have to be that way because they are being so careful.

If a man wanted to have sex with you tonight what would he do?

There would have to be an extreme level of attraction or a lot of alcohol, preferably both. If it's a one night stand he's got to have a lot to offer. I mean that physically and in how he satisfies me. Sex is the one area where I don't go out with doorknobs. The men that I sleep with are confident, outgoing and attractive.

What do you think guys need to know about having one night stands with women?

The biggest thing men need to realize is that sometimes sex is just sex and this applies to women too. The next morning, most guys are like, "Oh my god I think we have a relationship now." For me it's like, "No honey, you can leave now." It's a two way street. There are a lot of women with huge sex drives out there. Women are ten times as raunchy in conversation about men than you can ever imagine.

I have a theory that men are the romantic ones. Everyone always thinks that women are the romantic ones. Women are always the ones being cast as the sensitive emotional types. It's true, we probably are more ruled by our emotions, but it doesn't necessarily mean we are more romantic. I think it's all a big scam.

I think men are the romantic ones since they have such a romantic or overly romanticized view of what a woman is. They think a woman is this soft and flower kind of romance novel. When it comes right down to it, we are much more practical than men. In a romantic relationship, women are ten times more practical.

The other half of the theory applies to why men fear commitment. They fear commitment because they have much more of an idealized view of what a commitment is. For men, a commitment to a woman means that they are going to make this woman the center of their universe. She is like the end all and be all and this is going to be the person they are going to love forever. Everything revolves around her and they even put her up on a pedestal.

The reason why men are so skittish when they are making a commitment is because they want to be sure they are making the commitment to the right person. Whereas women view it as much more a partnership or an enhancement of their life, not an end all and be all. For women, relationships don't mean that they necessarily lose the rest of their lives. Women are more practical in this sense than men. I think men need to realize that if they put a woman on a pedestal she will fall off.

What do men need to know about having one night stands?

If men want to have one night stands then they definitely have to project the confidence. Men need to be like, "Okay, I can give you such a night." The best line ever given to me was given to me by this guy who came up behind me and whispered in my ear with the utmost confidence, "I want to make wild passionate love to you all night long," that was amazing. It was really effective with me because the guy was so confident. The confidence in what you say to a woman is everything.

With my last couple of one night stands I talked to the guy for at least a couple of hours of working it, there was definitely a spark. If you want to get laid tonight you need persistence, patience, focus and attention. Having those qualities will definitely pay off.

Name:	Terri
Age:	20
Occupation:	Hotel manager
Relationship Status:	Single

What is romance?

Romance to me is candlelight dinners, or a walk on the beach. A walk in the park under the stars, or being alone at home with the person cuddling, things like that.

How do you feel when those things happen?

I feel good. It makes me feel more loved and wanted than any other thing like going out. Going out and doing things is fine and fun, but romantic things make me feel like the man is taking time to care and to show me his emotions and feelings.

If you were giving advice to a close male friend about dating, what would you tell him to do?

First of all, I would tell him to be straight up and honest with the woman. He should tell her exactly what he wants. Don't play games with her, show her you are serious.

Look at the person. I can't explain the look, it would be that smile in that look that some guys have. That look that says, "I'm interested, but I don't know how to say it." Like a shy kind of glance and a smile. Flirt openly! If the girl has any sense, she will catch on. If she likes you she will flirt back; if she doesn't, she won't. If she doesn't, don't pursue it. If she does, talk to her, get to know her, like who the real "her" is. And then decide if you want to take her out and if you do just tell her.

What would your ideal lover be like?

He would be very romantic. He would also have a passionate needy side, like he couldn't wait. He would be spontaneous and sexually dangerous. He wouldn't care what anyone else thought. So, if he wanted to make love outside in the middle of the street, he would just do it. He would be tall, dark and handsome, built well, but not a muscle man. And he would have a nice smile.

Name:	**Shelly**
Age:	**47**
Occupation:	**Vocal teacher**
Relationship Status:	**Single**

What qualities do you look for in men?

He has to be very intelligent and open to a very eclectic variety of things. I need someone like myself. I am extremely intelligent, literate and successful in my field. I have tended to be drawn to men who are not as successful as me. In the relationship in which I loved the most, the man was very successful. He was very famous in his field. He was a brilliant musician.

What qualities do you need in a man to be in a serious relationship with?

I need a man who is responsible for himself, not a wanna-be. He knows who he is and where he is going. A man who already has his profession and knows what he is doing. Someone who loves what he does and whose work makes him happy.

A man who is not happy with his work is emotionally dangerous, because a man who is not happy with his work is usually not happy, period. A man's work is so important to him. If he is not doing the work he wants to be doing and wants to be doing something else, then he is emotionally dangerous to be around.

I just don't want any part of a man like that. He has to be honest and truthful and monogamous. I don't want any more shit about other women. I don't want to deal with it. I'd rather be alone.

116

Do you go out on dates often?

I don't want to go on a fucking date. I want a partner. I don't want to waste anymore time. If I want to go on a date, I'll go out with someone who is a real friend. I don't want to go on a date, I want to be with a man. I just want to go up to a guy and say, "Hi, do you want to have a monogamous relationship or not? If not, get the fuck out of here." I am just at that point.

I realize that I don't need a man who is my equal. I need a man who is a little beyond me. Because my equal could become some sort of competition. I need someone who is beyond me.

I used to think things like the guy being on time, telling the truth and bringing me flowers were a big deal. I now believe that if he doesn't do all those things, I don't even want to know him. I don't want to waste my time. He has to be on time. He has to tell the truth. He has to be responsible. He has to not waste my time.

I don't even want to deal with a man who doesn't have those qualities. I don't have any patience left. I don't want to be his mother. Shelly's finishing school is closed. This time around I just want to have fun. If you have problems, deal with them somewhere else.

What are turns-offs in men? What won't you put up with?

I don't want a man with sexual problems. I need someone who is free with his sexuality. I need someone who I don't have to worry about who he is flirting with.

I meet a lot of men who are not generous enough with me. They are stingy. I want a man who likes to be generous with me.

What is your advice for men?

Get your shit together, really get your shit together, do it for yourself. The biggest complaint that women have about men is that they are immature. They don't act like men, they tend to act out. Get over it already, handle it and be responsible. Be in the world, create something with yourself. To me, the men who are the most attractive are the ones who are open and honest and not playing games.

Men and women are different. We don't speak the same language. I think men should take the time to understand what women are like and what we need. We really do need all the little things taken care of; that's what makes us feel safe.

I really think that a problem with the American male is that he is so irresponsible as a rule, but there are individual exceptions.

I went to a seminar where they said that men were supposed to bring three things to a relationship: fun, sex, and clarity or certainty. Clarity and certainty go together, that is what a man is supposed to bring. He also has to be clear. The woman brings vision and that's it, men don't need anything else. He doesn't need to be in a relationship the way a woman does. He needs her vision. Women can see things and men are focused on one thing at a time.

I think the fear of commitment is total bullshit. People can't commit to someone else because they are afraid to commit to themselves. Women are always saying that men are afraid to commit. I don't have that fear. Whatever I take on, I take on balls to the wall. I need someone who will put his chips on the table and play full out.

Chapter 4: Professionals

Roni Raye Productions

120

Chapter 4: Professionals

In any industry, it's safe to assume that the professionals know more than the average person about their work. After all, it's their area of expertise. With this in mind, I interviewed many women in the sex industry. I interviewed strippers, phone sex operators, dominatrixes, online cybersex models, and sexual performance artists.

These women have a unique perspective on men. They have access to men's fantasies, desires, secrets, and vulnerabilities. They are in touch with the primal side of men, and have first-hand experience with hundreds of men. Perhaps they are jaded by the industry, or perhaps they know what they are talking about. You decide.

Name:	**Roni Raye**
Age:	**29**
Occupation:	**Amateur porn star, phone sex operator, model and more**
Relationship Status:	**In a long term relationship**

How long have you been in the porn business?

Over three years now. Before this I was working as a dental assistant. One day I got bored with the job and have been doing this ever since. I enjoy this so much because I get so much attention from men. My exposure is very different than a stripper, where they get immediate attention. I get the attention I crave, but I do it on my terms. I get letters, phone calls, but there is no physical contact with anyone.

What magazines have run photos of you?

Velvet, Gallery, Genesis, Cheri, Hustler's Busty Beauty, Amateur Hour, and many more.

How did you gain national attention?

I got national attention when the company I work for had legal problems from porn videos they were marketing. As a result of their legal battles, they received a lot of talk show footage on television. The company got lots of requests to be on talk shows. They asked me to be on Maury Povich with them. Once I was on Maury Povich and since I've been in all the magazines and had my photos in bookstores, I couldn't help but gain national attention. It doesn't mean that I am a national figure or anything. Guys who are definitely into pornography and way into the amateur industry will know who I am.

Do you enjoy doing professional phone sex?

I love it. I will probably be doing that until I am 80 or 90. I really like interacting with people. On a sexual level, it is very stimulating. It is not just about words, it is really fun. Contrary to people's beliefs, there are different types of phone sex operators. There are the big offices called boiler rooms, that have 500 girls working and you can hear phones ringing in the background. There cannot be a sexual connotation in those circumstances. The women are not for real, they are faking.

Then there is someone like myself, who works out of her home and lays in bed and does calls. There are certain men I have a connection with and it can be very sexual without faking.

Do you sometimes masturbate on calls?

Yes, I do. For someone who interviews women on sex, you sure get embarrassed.

I am not embarrassed at all. I am just trying to get my questions answered. Are you monogamous with your boyfriend?

By nature I am a monogamous person; I'm not a swinger. Many people think that because I do all the videos and phone sex, that I am a swinger, but I'm not. I only do videos with men I am in a relationship with, and you won't find that often. Most people who are doing porn videos or amateur videos are swingers, or have had multiple partners. The most men I've been with is only two.

Who are the men who call your phone sex line?

On my phone line I get doctors, lawyers, even Congressmen. I get people of all kinds who want to talk to me. I can't tell you which Congressmen I get, but I do. I get very influential and wealthy publishers. I don't know what makes me special, it is not just about sex. I have no problem with some guy calling me because he is horny and just wants sexual relief, because I enjoy that. I get power in doing that, it really builds my ego. There is something about hearing a man come on the other line that just gets me excited.

Have you had one night stands?

Not many. I have not been with too many men. I have only been with nine men in my life. I hate to say this and it sounds so contrary, but I was raised in a strict Baptist family. To me eight people is a sin, it is a lot of guys. Then again, some people think it is nothing.

Roni Raye Productions

I don't regret sleeping with anyone. Some were really good lays. Some were the result of drinking. I was just drunk, horny and wanted to fuck. Somewhere along the way I grew up.

Tell me about domination.

Most men won't admit that they like to have their ass played with, or that they like to have anything inside their ass. My boyfriend likes to be fucked in the ass with a strap-on dildo. I put on the thing and fuck him in the ass. He loves it. He goes nuts about it and he's totally heterosexual.

I think couples should talk more openly about what turns both of them on sexually and be open to doing what they can to please each other. Most women could not deal with it if their boyfriend asked them to fuck him in the ass with a strap-on. Most women would tell him to get the fuck out of the house and not come back. To me though, all the role reversal things are fun.

Are you sexually dominant with your boyfriend?

I am into being dominant, even with my boyfriend. I like to take the dominant position and he can be dominant on a personal level where he likes to be the man. But when it comes to fucking, I have him trained. He is my little sex slave. I am pretty sure of myself and know what I want at this point, and I am not afraid to tell a man about it.

How frequently do you have sex with your boyfriend?

As often as possible. On average, once a day and sometimes two or three times a day. Some days not at all.

The question I get asked the most is, given that I work in the sex industry and I am around it all the time, don't I get tired of it? No, it just doesn't happen with me, it actually helps out my sex life with boyfriend.

The phone sex company I work for also offers live sex calls. When I get those, I really have sex with my boyfriend. We put the guy on the speaker phone and he can interact with us. He can do anything he wants. I am telling him what I am doing to my boyfriend. I can hear him jacking off. It is like having a threesome. It can be pretty stimulating.

What are some of the unusual things you have done in videos?

I've done golden showers, brown showers, I've done it all. I've masturbated outdoors for a video. I've done it in way off places like a park, a grocery store, and while walking down the street. I do custom videos for guys. On another video I flashed guys on the street while wearing a strap-on dildo. I was sitting on a picnic table facing traffic going 65 miles per hour flashing them my tits and lifting up my skirt, showing off the strap-on. Cars honked at me. It was fun.

What is the difference between amateur and professional porn?

Amateur means a lot of things. It means that I look like the girl next door; I don't have a perfect body. I am not Playboy material. Amateur means that it is not on a professional set. It is not professionals doing it, it is spontaneous. That is why amateur videos are hot sellers, because people want to see what is real. Amateur videos are outselling the professional videos. It is a big industry.

What are some unusual experiences you have had in the porn business?

There was a guy who would send come in his letters to me. That was always interesting. I would try to open up the letter and it would have come all over it. I would get out my gloves and throw the letter away instantly.

What advice do you have for men who want to be more sexually experimental with their girlfriends and wives?

Communication is the key. However, you can communicate all you want and if you are not with the right person, then it isn't going to work. No amount of communication is going to work if the person was brought up with and still retains a strict Christian ethic and thinks sex is dirty. But, I think that if you are honest, but phrase it without trying to freak them out, then you have a better chance of having it happen.

You have to approach it in a gentle and caring way. If you experiment with a gentle approach, where she has control over whether she can do it or not, then she is more likely to try it. Too many guys don't think before they talk, they just blurt it out because they want it so badly. If guys would think about it ahead of time, decide how to phrase it, and ask the woman if she is willing to experiment with something, then they would be more likely to have it happen.

What signals do you give a guy when you are interested in him?
I am a big flirt and am very forward. I will make comments to guys if I'm interested. When I see something I like, I go for it. I like all different kinds of guys; I like shy guys and I like aggressive guys. But I don't like guys who are so aggressive that they are all over me.

If we spend the evening together and he doesn't make a move, I will. Maybe I will touch his hand or leg. If I am feeling good I will call him sweetie or honey. I've been known to grab men and kiss them. I like hugging; I am very affectionate.

People think that someone who does what I do for a living is a slut. They see the stereotypes. If you met me and didn't know what I do for a living, you would not believe it. I like living a double life.

What is your advice for men on how to meet women to date?
First of all, a man who goes out to meet a woman should not try to act like he is someone else, because women smell that. So many guys will see a particular woman and they will make a judgment call about what type of person she is and try to act like someone they think she would like. It goes on all the time. If a man is himself and the woman doesn't like him for himself, fine, go on to someone else. Too many

relationships begin in false pretenses. If a guy tries to trick women and not show his real desires and wants, she will eventually find out that he has been lying to her. Women obviously do it too.

It seems to me that men try to impress women because they are in such high demand. Men think they have to impress a woman to get her attention because who they are is not good enough to get her without the extra push to impress.

But that is the insecurity. If you didn't feel insecure and just went up, regardless of whether you thought you would measure up to her, and just started talking and were just you, you might be surprised at what happens. A lot of guys are very intimidated by women whom they think are out of their league. I can understand why they do it.

So you have no problem walking up and talking to a man you are interested in?

I get shy. I am a very shy person by nature, believe it or not. I am very shy. I have all kinds of insecurities going on. If I see someone I think is out of my league, I would just as soon not say anything as opposed to going up to him. But if he is next to me, I will talk to him.

Where do your women friends go if they want to meet a guy to date?

Nowadays, a lot of women I know are placing personal ads. I always tell everyone to do that. Run a personal ad in your local paper, stating everything you are looking for. Have the girls send you a picture or letter about themselves. Have them send their phone number and then see if you like them before you go out with them. If they want to see a rock band, that is a good place. Carnivals in the summertime are also good. Lots of people hang out in places like that. As you get older, the places you hang out seem to shrink and it gets harder to meet people. Online is good because you can write back and forth and get to know each other that way. If you want to meet someone quick, you have to go to bars. Get out and socialize. I guess singles dances and things like that are good, too. There are also singles meeting groups.

It is a big deal to approach a stranger and talk to her and get her phone number.
I understand that. I agree. I am not shy when I drink, but I don't do that anymore. I don't go out looking, either. I have various ways of satisfying myself.

What are these mysterious ways?
Masturbation is a good one. My trusty vibrator always works. I sometimes use it on calls.

There is no doubt about it, it is difficult to meet people these days. I can't tell you how many men call me up and ask me this question all the time. I always tell them to write an ad. When people write things down, they tend to be more real with who they are, rather than when they verbalize it. In a bar it is hard to go up to a woman and say, "Hi, my name is John. I am a single 28-year old male and I want to be spanked."

So you don't think there is some magical solution to the dating problem?
No way. If someone tells you they have the magical solution, then they are lying.

Is romance important to you?
Absolutely, I have to be romanced. Romance has always been important to me. The majority of women find romance to be crucial. A woman needs to feel important. She needs to feel that the guy has a genuine interest in her, enough to romance her. It doesn't always have to be flowers. It doesn't always have to be that he actually buys her something, it can

be a massage. I will take that over flowers any day.

Do you believe in fate?

One hundred and twenty percent, I believe in fate. I am one of those romantic-thinking people who thinks that every pot has a lid. When there is someone out there meant for you, fate will bring you together. Most likely when you are *not* looking for someone is when you will find them. When you are looking, you are looking too hard and you can't find anyone. When you are not looking, it gets you when you least expect it. I truly believe that if it is meant to be, it will happen and you will know it. I wish there was a magical solution. Someone is dating all the beautiful women. Maybe they are not any happier than you. But what are you supposed to do, change your whole personality to get these women? That's not right.

Men think they want to date strippers, porn stars, or whatever, and once they do, they realize that they didn't want it to begin with. Some of them get too jealous and can't handle it. Some of them don't realize they have to share her.

Roni Raye can be contacted at P.O. Box 502210, Indianapolis, IN 46250, E-mail: roniraye@indy.net. View her on the World Wide Web at: http:// www.fdbbs.com/roniraye.htm

Name:	**Nikki**
Age:	**33**
Occupation:	**Professional dominatrix**
Relationship Status:	**In a relationship with 2 men and 1 woman**

What qualities do you look for in the men and women you are sexual with and date?

I mostly look for sincerity, and of course, an interest in the lifestyle. I don't have any interest at all in mainstream sex. I basically look for honesty and sincerity. My relationships have all the aspects of "plain vanilla" relationships; they just have the S/M aspect thrown in, too.

How does the S/M aspect transfer into your everyday life?

It transfers because I am always in control. I am not opposed to compromise. It is not just "my way or the highway," but I always maintain a sense of control.

Does that mean your partners are not allowed to disagree with you?

No, that is not a rule, but they seldom do.

How do people show you they are sincere?

This is a lifestyle for me. This is not a lifestyle for everyone, which is fine. For some people this is strictly foreplay; it turns them on and that's as far as it goes. For those in the lifestyle, it's not like they have to have an orgasm. If you are in the lifestyle, you are getting such a mind-fuck 24 hours a day. I am not saying that having an orgasm isn't great and nice, but you don't need to have the physical orgasm because you have it psychologically.

Is that what the lifestyle means to you?

Yes, that is what it means to me. It means different things to different people. I can't speak for everyone. I've been to many support groups when we discuss what it means to be a lifestyle person. Lifestyle to me is when you are constantly in role 24 hours a day. It's not that you are standing around wearing leather, expecting people to crawl around at your feet. It's a mind-set. Sometimes it is much more relaxed than other times, but it is always there. To the outside world, me and my partners would appear to be a mainstream couple.

I don't order my slaves around unless we are in a full scene mode. They do what I ask them to do. I don't say, "Get your coat on and go to the store." I say, "Could you please go to the store and get this for me?" I love them. I have a lot of respect for them. I don't treat them like dirt.

How does being of part of the lifestyle influence the way you think and interact with people?
I think everyone should have the right to do whatever they want, or feel, to do. This is what I like to do, but not everyone else does. That is fine. I am not interested in mainstream things at all.

Occasionally I attend mainstream events because of my kids. I was in a coffee clutch recently with a bunch of vanilla moms. They were complaining about their husbands and sounded so powerless. I was just sitting with my mouth shut, thinking of all the ways I could train their boring husbands. To me, what they all do and think, is incredibly boring.

What is the most difficult thing about this lifestyle?
The hardest part for me is that I have kids. I have to maintain the lifestyle without giving anything away to them. Sometimes it ruins the spontaneity of things. But I am divorced, and my ex-husband usually has the kids on weekends.

Are you nasty and aggressive with the men who come to see you for sessions?

It depends, not everyone enjoys that. To give someone your submission is an erotic power play. It's the giving up of control that is very comforting. The majority of my clients have very controlling jobs. They give orders all day long. They are constantly in control and are constantly on top of things. They have very demanding positions and there comes a point where they just want to let it go. It's a wonderful place to be, and you get there in your own head. You worry about nothing. You give yourself to me, and I make all the decisions.

Do you normally beat the men who come to see you?
I flog them, not all the time with each guy. I flog them, spank them, tie up their testicles and put clamps on their nipples. I do a lot of things.

What is your favorite thing to do, or one of your favorites?
Probably spanking. I love spanking.

Do you spank them until they beg you to stop?
When I spank them for pleasure I do it until they are bright red. They usually don't beg me to stop.

How long does it usually take to get their butt bright red?
It depends on their skin. Usually between one and five minutes of intense spanking.

Do you tie them up during the process?
Sometimes I tie them up, and other times I put them across my knee.

What are some of the other options?
They can be tied to an X-rack, or over a saw-horse.

What goes through your mind when you are spanking them?
I get a rush, but I don't get it with everyone. Sometimes
there isn't a connection. I get a charge out of basically having
psychological control. The physical part does very little for
me. I enjoy the psychological part. I am somewhat of a sadist
and I love to watch people squirm in pain. But that's not the
biggest part for me. The big part is knowing that I am in
control and knowing that they are letting me do what I want,
because it pleases me.

What are you thinking when you are dominating someone?
I am thinking that they are getting what they deserve.

What are some extreme things you've done to guys?
I once hung a fifteen pound weight from a guy's testicles. At
the same time, I had the guy on his toes with his nipples
strung up on a winch. So he was being pulled in both
directions.

So what was his response to that?
He just thanked me.

Did he cry?
He was close, but he enjoyed it. It is one of those love/hate
relationships. With the pain you hate it, yet you love it at the
same time.

*What did you do when he was standing there in pain? Did you just
watch him, talk to him, or what?*
I talked to him.

What did you say to him?
I asked him how that made him feel, and I told him that he
deserved the pain I was giving him. I also told him that he
knew he got himself into this situation. It would depend on

the person, but I would tell him things of that nature.

How many men have you seen?
Hundreds.

Annie Sprinkle

For the past 22 years, Annie Sprinkle has been involved in the sex industry. She started as a 42nd Street dancer. Later, she was a porno star and prostitute in massage parlors. She has contributed numerous articles and photographs to porn magazines.

In 1985 she moved into the world of performance art. Since then, she has performed all over the world. She has consistently broken taboos and pushed the limits with her performances. In a number of shows she invited the audience to inspect her cervix with a speculum and flashlight. Since then, she has turned her attention to writing books, including *Post Porn Modernist*, and *Metamorphosex*.

What advice do you have for men about dating women?

Sexuality is very important and that is my area of expertise. When you are approaching someone you don't know whom you want to date, I would say not to project your sexual energy and desires out there, but keep moving it. Circulate it in your own body and use it to charge yourself.

There are a lot of guys who are looking to date. They might be single or might not have had sex for a while, they might have a lot of sexual energy. I would say to keep circulating it in your own body and don't be needy.

Love yourself, that's the most important thing. Really learn to love yourself so that you come to a woman in your power and strength, feeling strong and good about yourself. A lot of guys are looking for a woman because they need something. Women sometimes react to that in a negative way. So be strong in yourself. Really take good care of yourself, love yourself and give to yourself. Fulfill your own needs and then you can be with a woman for who she is. Then whatever she wants to give you is enough. You are not needy. The worst taboo is to be needy.

Annie Sprinkle

Do you think guys in general are needy?

There are guys who are just single and busy with things, and they might need a woman that they like. Dating sounds like you are going after something rather than enjoying something that is there.

Do the romantic things, give her flowers; that's always good. Be in it for what you can give, not for what you can get and you will get a lot more.

Do you ever find yourself wanting to date someone new or go out just to meet someone?

No, I never date. I'm a married monogamous lesbian.

What would you do if you broke up?

I would always be interested in meeting new people. But I try not to be needy. That's the worst, it turns people off. People don't use that word "dating" much anymore. I would say "going out with" or "getting together," but not "dating."

Name:	**Mistress Mona**
Age:	**38**
Occupation:	**Professional dominatrix**
Relationship Status:	**In long term relationship for the past 10 years.**

What qualities do you look for in the men you date?

Intelligence, sense of humor, sense of sarcasm, the ability to keep up with me mentally, and someone that is non-macho in stereotypical terms. I hate the typical macho attitudes.

Sexually, I am monogamous to one man. I am around a lot of men all the time. Being a dominatrix, I have very close and intimate relationships with men of different socioeconomic categories and classes. Generally, a submissive male who likes a dominant female is from a very high educational background, has a high income level, and is in a leadership or power position in his career. I tend to see men who have a lot of pressure in their lives.

How long have you been a dominatrix?

I've been dominant since the day I was born. I have been controlling men all of my life. I have been a professional dominatrix on and off for ten years.

Were you controlling men when you were a kid, and when you were in high school?

It's not controlling as the mainstream society looks at it. There is a difference between domineering and domination. I am a very aggressive and independent female, versus being a woman who wants the husband or the man to take care of everything. I know what I want, and I don't wait around waiting for someone to give it to me. I go out and get it.

How is your relationship with your boyfriend structured? How does it compare with a mainstream dating situation?

We are equal in our relationship. On an everyday basis, we are equal in our relationship. He has his areas, I have mine. I am the stronger personality. I am the more aggressive and dominating personality. He pretty much bows down to whatever I want to do, whatever I want to partake in. He gives me whatever I want.

How is it possible for you to have an equal relationship with him if you ultimately have power and control?

I totally love and adore him, and he knows it. The girls I know tell me they can see it in his eyes when he looks at me.

What does it take to get you lustful and passionate?

I find different things in different people. The more I can get a response, the hotter it makes me. It can be complete arousal, whimpering, moaning, begging, tears, or it can be screams of pain. If I can extract a genuine response from someone, then that does something for me. You have to have the chemistry, too.

Men should understand the mental aspect. Men are more inclined toward the visual aspect than women are. Women are not visual people. You should understand the mind fucks. I like having power, having an effect on someone. Without the mental interaction, it doesn't happen. In this particular lifestyle you have to understand both roles. You have to see it; you have to feel it, it's not something that can be easily described.

What is your typical session like with a man?

I specialize in forced feminization. I work with cross dressers, humiliation, medium to heavy pain, flogging and bondage. I don't get into other areas.

What do you specifically do during a session?

It depends on the person. It is not always one way. With one of my cross-dressers, they may need to be taken shopping. They may be need taken into Victoria's Secret and it may need to be announced to the sales clerk that we're here to purchase things for this little slut. Or it may be an afternoon of cleaning my house, or giving my dog a bath, or polishing my shoes. It doesn't always include pain, and not everyone is into pain. Not everyone is into corporal punishment or varying degrees of discipline.

What goes into your decision to make someone shine your shoes?

It depends on the personality I am dealing with. The general image is that if you are a dominant woman, everybody's going to do exactly what you want to do, no matter what your desires or needs are. That is not the case with me; it may be with other people. I look for what that person needs.

There are different types of dominants. I am a mental dominant into sensuality, rather than what we call stripper dominants or commercial doms.

What is the difference?

A stripper dom is some little sleaze-bag escort or lingerie model who has decided to cash in on a market that she knows nothing about. The type of men she caters to are guys who have the fantasy of a woman overpowering them sexually. A commercial dominant learns all the ropes, no pun intended, opens up a commercial house and does it only for a living. She doesn't necessarily have that female supremacist attitude and basis. She is doing it only for the money.

What is a female supremacist attitude?

I believe that females are superior to men. If you ask me for proof of that, I will tell you that I don't have proof for that, it is my opinion. It is my attitude.

Can you tell me more about that idea?

Men are lead by their hormones, women are not. Every female is born with the power to control a man. Not every female learns to utilize that power in a positive manner. A lot of females learn to use that power in a malicious manner, to hurt. I don't believe in that. We can control, we can extract the things we want. We can instill in our males adoration and worship without hurting them, by feeding them what they need.

Is that how you respect and love men?

I adore men. I am not a man-hater at all. They are precious, precious creatures.

What is your opinion on female slaves and submissives?

There are many slaves and submissives, and they are usually taken by the male dominants, which I laugh at. They crack me up because they are not into the mental aspects of it; they are into the physical aspects only. It is something you would assume a male is going to do. I am talking about the mental control over their slaves rather than barking out orders and having someone do things out of fear. Generally, what I see is that they control by intimidation. They instill fear into their slaves. They don't do it with love. They do it because they have the physical power, not because they have the mental power.

What do you think about men who have the fantasy to be a dominant rather than submissive?

Are they having the fantasy or are they living the life? I don't fantasize about being dominant, because I am. They are probably dealing with overbearing women in their life all the way around.

Let me give you an example of a man who seeks out domination. This is a classic example. The man has gotten up in the morning, he has kicked his dog on the way down the stairs, he is in a bad mood, he screams at his kids, he bitches at his wife, he grabs his briefcase, he sits in traffic all morning long, when he gets to his office he has to lay off half of his staff because of cut-backs, he has to cut somebody else's contract, he has to fight his way home through traffic, and get back home and do it all over again.

He feels guilt for these things. He feels bad for the things society has forced him into doing because he is a male, because he is in a leadership position, because he has power. It may not be what he wanted to do, but he was forced into it by means that are uncontrollable by him.

He feels that he needs to atone for what he feels is a sin, and the way he possibly does that is by being beaten, being controlled, being humiliated, being forced to wear a pink tutu with white tights, it could be a myriad of things. Men have been put into positions that a lot of them don't necessarily want to be in. Many men tell me that, but they probably won't tell you that. They don't necessarily want to be the ones in control all the time. They don't necessarily want to have all that power all the time, but society dictates that they have to have it.

How do you train men?

You are not going to believe this. I train them as if they were women; I teach them what it's like. They have to learn to do manicures and pedicures. One of my slaves who is being seriously trained has to wear bras with water balloons in them. He is given a schedule to follow. He wanted to learn how to serve completely and totally. I took his request and ran with it. If he wants to really understand and serve properly, he has to know what it feels like to be a woman. He takes a lot of things upon himself that are not ordered by me. A lot of times he is required to wear those water balloons frozen.

Does he have a daily routine?

Absolutely. He has something to do every day. Right now he is learning to apply nail polish without getting it glopped up. He has to paint his toe nails at least three times a week. He has to learn how to take care of delicate and pretty little feet by taking on his own, because men have tougher skin and more calluses. If he can take care of his own feet, then of course he can take of his goddess' feet properly. He is also very much into feeling restrained and feeling like he can't get away, so he is required to sleep in certain things, one of which is a Saran-Wrap skirt. He wants a wife. He wants a woman he can dedicate himself to.

How long will it take you to train him?

With this particular person, it shouldn't take me long because the desire and curiosity is there. He goes a little farther than necessary. For instance, when I told him he had to wear the water balloons, he took it upon himself to find the perfect type of balloons that would hold the water best for freezing. He also experimented with different sizes of balloons. He will take a command or an idea that I give him and he will run with it. He is exceptional. He is what I call a total submissive.

Could you tell if a man was totally submissive just by looking at him?

I certainly would know very quickly. I could see it in how his body moved around females. I give submissive men credit for being the way they are. They are more worthy than the average straight male because they wants to learn. They want to make someone happy. They want to serve.

What happens when a submissive sees you? He pays to see you and then what?

I don't like to talk about money that crudely.

How would you put it?

He supports his goddess. The gift of submission is very precious. It is one of the greatest gifts in the world.

What are the emotional and psychological changes you see in men after they've seen you for a long time?

They learn to be more aware of their actions. They become more aware of what they do and what is going on around them. For instance, I was at lunch the other day with a very dear friend of mine. She had a slave with her. He adores her and worships her. She never had to stir her own glass. Every time my glass was refilled the Sweet 'n' Low was automatically put in the glass and stirred. My cigarettes were put out for me; I didn't have to do that.

Through his training he has learned to be aware of everything that is going on. He has also learned to be sure that his goddess is comfortable, and that she is happy and well taken care of.

How does she reward him for that?

Through her attention, her love and affection.

How long do your sessions last?

It all depends on the individual. Some people keep their slaves over the weekend.

What do they do over the weekend?

They lock them up at night in cages. They may be there to serve over the weekend. They may have certain chores they have to do. They might be there to serve at a party, to serve as a house boy or as a serving wench.

Do your subs please you sexually?

No, that never happens. That is what I have a love slave for. I know dominatrixes who never allow their submissives to release, and I know some who are offended if they don't. Some of my submissives are not allowed to masturbate unless they have my permission. Men have always been my playthings.

Do you ever engage in golden showers?

I will if someone begs hard enough, and I have to go bad enough. It is a common fetish. I once had a client who loved dirty and sweaty women. The more stinkier, sweatier and dirtier the better. All he wanted to do was talk about these women.

I had another guy who wanted me to fart in his face. That has got to be the strangest one I have come across. I am not judging the guy, but I just can't figure out where the hell that would come from. Probably as a child, his sister would hold him down and fart on him, or something like that.

These are areas I don't do because they are of no interest to me. If I am not interested in them, then I can't do them any justice. I don't deal with adult babies or blood sports. I am here to provide assistance, not steal their money.

What are your common sexual fantasies?

My fantasy, when I was 18 and continuing this day, is to have an island where I could select all the male workers by hand. I would line them up like a drill sergeant would, put on my boots and walk up and down the line. I would select and deselect the men I wanted to keep, getting rid of the inferiors. It is a common fantasy among dominant women.

Professionals

What are some odd things you have made slaves do?

I have some slaves who take on the persona of an animal.
They are precious. I had one for a short period of time that
was a German shepherd named Spike, and he was a very
good dog. He would play ball with his mistress; he would
run and fetch. He was very subservient: If I would be sitting,
he would be kneeling next to me. I wouldn't even have to
move my cigarette to flick my ashes; he would make sure
they were flicked off into his hand. He had a dog dish.

*That would strike me as kind of funny. I would probably laugh at
someone who was doing that.*

I just find it really cute. I love animals, that may be part of it.
I love dogs. I don't know the reason behind it, but I've seen
it several times. They are usually very precious. They are
usually very sweet and docile, but if someone gets near their
mistress, they growl. They take on an entire dog persona. I
would also make them go outside to pee, it is more of a
subservient thing. Spike liked to curl up at my feet. He was
very content curled up at my feet.

Sexpectations

Chapter 5: The Primal Years

Sexpectations

Chapter 5: The Primal Years

A few months into writing this book, I noticed that most of older women I was interviewing were very sexually active. I had always read that women in their 40's have a dramatic increase in sexual desire. Sometimes their sexual desires are compared with those of adolescent boys. I wasn't surprised at their level of sexual desire and frequency. I was surprised, however, that so many older women were becoming involved in bondage, dominance and submission, and other "kinky" sex, and had gotten into it rather recently. I was intrigued and fascinated at what could be happening inside them to bring on such a radical shift in lifestyle and desire at such an age.

My interviews uncovered a few commonalties of experience. First, their children were finally grown and had moved away from home. Second, these women had enjoyed various fantasies since they were girls, but had never felt comfortable expressing them until recently. Somehow, turning 45 (or whatever age) set them free from caring what other people might think of them. Finally, these women have a high level of self-acceptance and regard for getting on with life.

The women interviewed are all professionals. Their occupations range from legal secretary to corporate CEO. Among them, they have some wild experiences and unorthodox opinions about sex. More than any other group of women I spoke with, the primal years women tended to be open, intelligent and funny. They are wonderful communicators, easy to talk with, and well beyond trying to hide or prove anything.

Read on and discover the secret world of women in the primal years.

Name:	**Liz**
Age:	**53**
Occupation:	**Casino worker on a gambling boat**
Relationship Status:	**In a committed relationship**

When did you begin experimenting with being a submissive?
About three years ago.

What was your sex life like prior to that?
For the nine years prior to my divorce, my sex life was nonexistent. I shut down my sexuality. I could never do that now.

Why do so many women become more sexually experimental in their late 40's and early 50's?
It's probably a mid-life crisis. For me, I was in a dead-end marriage. When I got online it was my salvation. I met a guy who was into D&S and he was much younger.

What is your relationship like with your current boyfriend?
He owns me, which means that he does whatever he wants whenever he wants, where he wants to, and however he wants to do it. In the absence of a direct instruction, I run my own life. He doesn't want somebody who needs to ask to turn on a light or other simple tasks. He wants basically self-maintaining people. When there is a question of who's in charge or who makes the decisions, if he has a feeling about something, then it is his voice that counts. If he asks me to do something and I just flat out don't think I can do it, our relationship is structured such that we can sit down and we try to reach some sort of a compromise. Everything between us is like a normal relationship except that when he wants to have sex, we have sex.

153

What if you don't want to do what he asks?
Tough luck.

How does that feel to know that he has that type of control over your body?
That's the whole erotic part of this relationship. The whole point is that I get turned on by being controlled.

What goes through your mind if he wants you to go to the store and shop for him and you don't want to go? What do you think when he orders you?
If it is going to be something that is going to be difficult, I have to reach deep inside myself and say, "Where is it written that being submissive is always fun?" And then I go do it anyway. It's very simple: submission is not a game. It's not something you turn off and on. It's a lifestyle, and in return for living a very erotic existence you pay your dues. It's like your job. If your boss tells you to do x, y or z, you may not want to do it, but you do it anyway because that is where your paycheck comes from.

The first decision a submissive makes is whether she is going to stop making decisions or not? Is she going to give up the ability to make decisions? Once you decide "Yes, this man owns me," then that is the last decision you make except to end the relationship.

What is your favorite way to be punished?
My current partner likes a cane, which is not necessarily what you walk with when you are 90. A cane in his case is a piece of graphite fishing rod which has the handle covered nicely with rubber. When he whips me the whip stings me; the pain is biting. My weapon of choice happens to be a flogger. In particular, I have one that is heavy leather and has about 20 strands and hits with a thud rather than a bite.

The amount of pain I can take is relative to the amount of

endorphins that are flowing through my body. It's like a runner's high. If you start out cold and just smack me with your flat hand it is going to hurt. If I work up to it you can hit me a lot harder and it will be okay.

My master has taken me to a place in sub-space where he had me literally frozen, completely frozen. He had me looking at my hand and recognizing that it wasn't my hand anymore, it was his hand. He definitely put me in an altered state of consciousness. He just took me there with his voice and instructions. He just told me that was happening. I am sure it was a variant of hypnosis or a form of being hypnotized. Beyond that, I really can't tell you what he did. I suspect that when I am in that state he can inflict a good deal of pain on me and I would recognize it as pain and not feel it as pain.

Are you turned on by public humiliation?

If, for example, I was in a mall with my master and he told me to get down and kneel beside him, I would do it and it wouldn't be humiliating. The reason it wouldn't be humiliating is that he is not doing it to make me feel bad. He is doing it to demonstrate his control over me and because I am doing what I have been told to do. I am proud of my submission. That's a whole different mind-set than being humiliated.

So you wouldn't feel embarrassed kneeling in a mall?

I probably would feel a little embarrassed, but I wouldn't feel humiliated.

What is the difference between dom-space and sub-space?

The difference between dom-space and sub-space is that dom-space is doing and sub-space is feeling. Obviously, being in dom-space for a master is a turn-on.

Name: Mary
Age: 47
Occupation: Buyer for a wholesale liquor distributor
Relationship status: Single

How did you get into D&S?

I don't like to call what I am into S/M or D&S. I am more of a sensual, loving, erotic player. A friend of mine said that if it has to be called S/M, I would rather call it "sensual manipulation." That fits perfectly.

When I started dating again, every man out there was only offering cheap, empty and meaningless sex. It didn't interest me until I discovered this form of sexuality.

There are relationships that form, and you choose your partners carefully. You plan out your strategies and know your limits. You know your likes and dislikes. It is kind of cold and calculating, but you still need a certain amount of chemistry between two people before they play. People into this type of sexuality become very intimate. You are totally vulnerable, especially when you are tied up or restrained or in a humiliating position of some sort. You are really exposing much more of your self than if you picked up a woman at a bar and took her home.

Are you always on top?
Definitely, I am a dominant.

Is it your goal to be in a monogamous relationship?
Yes, it definitely is.

What are the qualities you look for in the men you date?
I like intelligent men. Believe me, I have interviewed some men who were not very smart and they don't interest me. I

156

like a little bit of feistiness, a little bit of fight and a little playfulness. I like submissive men, but I do not totally humiliate them. I always maintain a level of respect for my partner. Professional mistresses often call guys every name in the book and just totally humiliate them because they really don't care about them. If I care about someone, I can't really be that mean or humiliating to that person. I need to maintain a level of respect for that person.

What do you do on dates?

When I meet someone for the first time we have a casual meeting first, a dinner, lunch, or a drink, something of that sort. It is an interview of sorts, after several phone conversations. In the meeting we will explore if we have the proper chemistry and if there is trust. If we like each other and there is a degree of lust and trust, then we will talk about playing. Possibly we would play that night, but usually later. I am not just looking for mindless zombie submissives who will clean my car and house. I want a relationship that is based on deep trust and intimacy.

How has what you've looked for changed over the past few years?

It has changed drastically. If you would have told me that I would be looking for what I am looking for now, I would have said you were crazy.

I just really get turned on by playing with men. I enjoy tying a man all up and playing with him, teasing him, taunting him, and tormenting him. I just love it so much. It is a wonderful turn on and so is being in control.

Five years ago you were just a vanilla girl?

Yes. I used to just lie on my back and spread my legs.

When you are with a man and you are tying him up, don't you get into any mild verbal abuse?

I am not into verbal abuse at all. I give straight orders. I just usually like the adoration aspect of the situation, like asking him who he adores, worships and loves, of course it is me.

What do you make your men wear?

They are naked for me. They usually wear a collar and I have a leash. They might wear a cock ring and harness. I have a little leash for the cock and balls. I like to have both leashes in my hand. I have restraints for the ankles and wrists. I have different lengths of chain and different lengths of cording to restrain them. I have a device where I can have a man bound in between my legs. I put them on their knees, tie their wrists together, blindfold them, tie their hands behind their back, and attach the collar to my thigh strap and tell them to pleasure their mistress.

If I were your slave and came over to visit you, would we ever talk out of character to each other?

At first we would talk normally. However, the minute we go into role, we go into role. You would know it because I would grab a collar and stick it on your neck. I would refer to you as "slave" and it would be time to go.

What sexual characteristics do you look for in a man?

I love men who are very oral and anal. I love to play with men's butts. How many women will tell you that? It has been a long road for me and I have been awakened. To have a man masturbate for me, that is the biggest turn on in the world for me.

I have absolutely no qualms about what I do. I will use a strap on and I will fuck a man in the ass. I will play with a whip. I will tease him, taunt him, spank him and flog him. I will even give him an enema. I have no bad feelings about anything I do, because everything is safe, sane and consensual. Much worse things are going on out there in supposedly "normal" relationships.

Do you ever masturbate for your men?
No, I like to have them do me. That is a big turn on, too. I especially like it when they pleasure me with my vibrator and they look up at me, watching me moan in pleasure. That is a huge turn on.

What does a man do if you are hurting him or playing with him in a way he doesn't enjoy?
We discuss that ahead of time. We discuss what his limits are and what he does and does not like. I have my own limits too. I will not engage in fecal play, there will be no branding, piercing, flaming, no drawing of blood, no severe pain or torture. There are people who are into that stuff, but I am not. I like the sensual and erotic aspects of dominance and submission.

What is the typical scene like when you are with a man? How do you set up the room and what is the ambiance like?
I usually light a lot of vanilla-scented candles. I play Gothic music. I set the mood. I don't have a leather outfit, but I usually wear a teddy or negligée, thigh-high nylons and heels. I want to look sexual and erotic.

The big thing in D&S is texture, it is about awakening the senses. I like to alternate play between hard things and soft things, feathers or lamb's wool or rabbit fur, and then ice cubes, candle wax, lotions, spanking. I like to alternate all kinds of sensations. Being tied up and blindfolded just heightens the sense of sensation, it increases the feelings in the body. It is really quite erotic. It is a teasing, a taunting, a fondling. It's a lot of fun.

What it comes down to is something that we should be doing much more in normal life, which is spending an enormous amount of time on our partner.

Name:	**Robin**
Age:	**42**
Occupation:	**Computer programmer,**
	corporate trainer
Relationship Status:	**Married**

What is your advice for men wanting to date?

Cut out some of the game playing. There are some girls out there who like nice guys. You don't have to be an asshole.

Do you think a lot of women want nice guys?

There are some girls who aren't happy unless they are being mistreated. You hear guys all the time say, "Women don't like nice guys. You've got to be a jerk, you've got to string them along." But that's not necessarily true. You probably shouldn't be so attentive that she can't turn around without you standing behind her, but there are plenty of women who appreciate a nice guy.

If a man approached you while you were out and about, would you like that? Would you find that flattering?

Yes, I do find it flattering. It is nice.

And do you talk back?

I flirt back.

How could a man approach you in a way that would make you feel comfortable and safe enough to date him?

He shouldn't be openly and blatantly sexual. Being crude is fun to play with, but it won't get you any women.

What would you think and how would you feel if a guy came up to you and said he thought you were beautiful?

I always wonder what they are up to. I've had it happen a few times. The trouble is that when men say that, they are usually not looking at my face, they are looking at my cleavage. It comes off just a wee bit insincere because my face is about eight inches up from where they are looking.

They don't even have to be terribly flattering. Just like, "Hi, I saw you and I find you very intriguing. You are very pretty, and I'd like to talk to you," stuff like that. I feel bad for guys having to do that. There are some mercenary bitches out there that are going to size you up for whether you are wearing a Rolex, or whether you have money. I feel bad for guys for usually having to be the aggressors.

What is your advice for men who just want to have one night stands?

If that is what your primary objective is, it isn't as easy as it used to be. At the same time, it isn't all that hard to do. It does take time and money. Most importantly, you have to be willing to settle for a certain class of girl.

What class is that?

Trailer trash.

Where do those type of women tend to hang out?

Bars are often full of them. Go to low rent kind of places.

How would you advise men to approach a woman in a bar?

The thing that seems to work best in a place like a bar is to flatter them and treat them like a lady, because they know damn well they're not.

How specifically would you flatter them?

Tell them how pretty they are and how impressed you are with them. Say stuff like, "I've always wanted to be with a girl like you. You are so pretty. It is so good to be with a nice girl." They know they are trash, but they like to hear that stuff like anybody else. Girls who really get off on that aren't really secure anyway.

How old are the women you are referring to?
They come in a variety of ages from late teens to late 50's.

What would it take for you to have an affair?
A really intriguing situation.

Have you been in an intriguing situation yet?
Over the past eight years it's happened a few times. I have
slept with six or seven people. A few times with another
woman and the rest with men.

Did your husband know what you were up to?
Sure he knew. It was no problem for him. He trusts me. I
could sleep with someone tonight and it would be no
problem for him.

Does your husband also have affairs?
He is really into bondage, discipline, and BDSM related
activities. He has had many adventures over the past few
years with other women.

How often does he have affairs?
He was a lot more into it before we were married. Now it
happens about four times a year. He is a very powerful man
and aggressive in his normal life. As a diversion he loves to be
a submissive. You would never know it by looking at him or
even living with him.

Do you dominate him?
Sometimes I do, but it is hard for me. I have a hard time with
the idea of the man who I depend on for strength on one
level to be so weak at times. I can do it sometimes, but it is
hard for me. That is why he ventures outside of our marriage.

What are some of the oddest things you have done sexually?
I watched a woman have sex with a dog.

Where did you see it done?
Right in front of me. Before I was married, I knew this girl who was into that and she had a rather aggressive male dog. Her big thing was to go down on someone, male or female, it didn't matter who, while her dog did her. And you've heard about dogs getting stuck? It's true they do.

Was she going down on you?
Yes.

When you play with other women, what do you do?
Tying them up is fun. The occasional woman who is into being whipped is fun.

Do you insult them or act out verbal abuse?
Sometimes. I make them expose themselves. There was this one woman who was into forced public exhibition. We used to drive around and go to truck stops and make her expose herself to truck drivers. We would make her take off her shirt or raise up her skirt. We'd go shopping with her with no underwear on. We didn't do it so kids or families would be offended, but we would give the occasional shoe salesman a show. That would totally turn her on. She enjoyed being forced into doing it. She was really shy about her body, so forcing her gave her an opportunity just to be herself.

Why do men focus so much on pleasing a woman? Men seem overly concerned with making a woman come, why do you think this is?
Men need to realize that a woman having an orgasm is not always the end result. Men always want to come, but it is different for women. Women can have good time and not come. Even sex that isn't all that good ain't usually that bad.

How much can you complain at the end of the day about a blow job?

Is sex like mental manipulation?

The biggest sex organ is your brain. Sometimes just getting into the right head space is what makes having an orgasm possible for a woman, not the physical stimulation.

How do you get into that space?

It depends on the situation. There is no tried and true method, but I have to feel like the guy really wants to be with me. If it's truly just physical sex, then you don't think, you just feel. But if it's a mental exercise, it depends on the person.

What is it like when you lose control?

If I am completely out of control it allows me to concentrate on total physical sensation. It's total hedonism, it really is.

Name:	**Anna Maria**
Age:	**42**
Occupation:	**Manager of computer programming firm**
Relationship Status:	**Divorced, currently single**

Does it turn you on to date younger men?

In my mind it does, but when I talk to younger men and they are interested, I want to say, "Are you sure you want to go out with me?" It is fine with me to date young men. I also try to rationalize it from his point of view. I try to think about why he would want to go out with me. However, lots of guys I meet like older women.

Why do you think that is?

Older women are more experienced. They know what they want and are sexually more experienced. I am sure that is a plus. They are more mature and have gotten past some things, like indifference. I am not sure how to describe it, but they don't have the need to latch onto someone. I think a lot of men are afraid of women being clingy or whatever.

When women are older, especially when they've already been married, they usually don't need a man. I think that piece of it makes it easier for men to relax around women and not be so worried about where they are trying to take them, or trying to manipulate them.

What are some unusual sexual experiences you have had?

I am sexually submissive, but when I started all of this, I thought I was dominant. I once placed an ad in a local newspaper looking for a submissive man to play with. It turned out to be very odd. That was definitely one of the most unusual experiences I have had.

What happened when you met the guy? What made the experience so unusual?

First of all, he begged me to do a session with him and I was very hesitant. Finally I decided to play with him because he begged me so much and called me so often. He wanted me to come over on Christmas Eve, and he lives about 45 miles away. He went on and on telling me how he would do whatever I wanted. I thought about it and said, "I don't really think that is my thing." In the end I thought I would just give it a try. I was amazed that I could even do it.

When I arrived at his home he was as I told him to be; naked, kneeling and waiting for me. I told him to lie on his stomach and I looked around his apartment.

What exactly did you do to him?

I didn't insult him and didn't hit him that much. I made him put on a dog collar and a leash. I first made him lie down while I checked out his apartment. I wanted to see where things were, and I decided just to make him wait for me. When I came back, I took him back into his bedroom. I tied him up to the bed and hit him with a riding crop. He was a total wimp and cried a lot. I hit him a few times and he started to cry really hard. He kept asking me to stop. I kept reminding him that he told me I could do anything to him that I wanted. I asked him so many times when I first got there if this is really what he wanted me to do and he responded, "Yes," every time.

What else did you do to this guy? Did you do cock and ball torture on the guy or anything like that?

No, not at all.

Something must have happened for him to have such a strong reaction.

I made him suck on my nipples. I had clothes pins and I put

166

them on his nipples and he whined about that. I put them on his balls and he really whined about that. Then I left him alone for a while. I went downstairs and got some ice cubes to touch his body with. When I came back in, he was upset. He was whining, so I took the clothes pins off him. I also had him blindfolded and I took that off as well. Then it was kind of abrupt because his roommate came home and he didn't expect her to be there for two more hours. And he was naked. I called him on the way home to see if he was okay and he didn't call me back. I called him a few times after that and he never got back to me.

And now you are always a submissive?
Yes, I haven't gone the other way ever since. In my head I've always been submissive. I only did it with that guy because he begged me to.

What are you thinking when you are tied up? What goes through your mind?
I just feel helpless. It is just a total turn-on. I do whatever the dom wants; it is different with each one.

Do you enjoy being spanked?
Spanking is good for me. I like things that are stimulating.

What is attractive to you about receiving pain?
I like not being in control. Since I was a child, I always knew that this was my way of being sexual.

What are some fantasies you have that have not been acted out yet?
A gang bang with lots of guys.

How many guys?
Probably five or six. I have another fantasy that I am being kidnapped and forced into slavery, something like that. Somebody grabs me and throws me into a car. He takes me

somewhere and says, "Here is your master. He now owns you." Those are the two I think about most often.

Name:	Cynthia
Age:	47
Occupation:	Administrative assistant
Relationship Status:	Single

What do you look for in the men you date?

I look for intelligence more than anything else. I also look for humor, a positive way of looking at things and someone who doesn't see the world as other people see it. I also look for honesty. I can't stand a dishonest man.

Do you date a lot?

I've been involved with a married guy for the past three years. I have also been dating a local guy for the past two years. My relationships tend to be long term.

Are you looking for a monogamous relationship?

It is really hard to say. My attitude towards sex is probably more male than it is female. I've had many relationships over the years. Most of the time it has been friendship and sex. I don't usually go for the big heavy relationships. I have fun with the men I date, and it stems from a mutual attraction and a desire to get them into bed.

Do you ever have one night stands?

Almost never. I can count them on one hand.

Do you like to be romanced?

Yes, but it is not a big priority. I was married for 20 years. I like to be treated well. I don't like it when men try to impress me by taking me out and wining and dining me. I don't go for that. I am more concerned with what he is like inside.

What's the best pickup line you have heard?

The most unique one was when a guy walked up to me as I was standing in line at the deli. I was married at the time. He lifted my hand up and said, "Those are really pretty rings." I said, "Thank you," and then he asked me if I was happily married. I said, "Funny you should ask, because my husband and I are separated right now." Then he said, "Great, so do you want to go out?" I said, "Sure." We went out and ended up dating for two months. He really caught my attention because I was completely not expecting it.

If you were giving a close male friend advice on how to meet women, what would you tell him?

I would tell him that meeting women is not hard to do. They are all around; the whole world is a shopping mall. Don't ever be afraid to show a woman that you honestly appreciate her company or conversation, that is the best way to go about it. You are going to get a lot farther telling a woman that you like the way her mind works than telling her she has pretty hair or a nice smile. Women want men who can do more than stroke their egos about their appearances; at least the older women do.

At what point during a date do you know if you will sleep with the man?

I usually know before I go out with him. If there is not something about him that attracts me sexually, I usually take pains to make sure it doesn't go anywhere.

The best lover I ever had was a guy you would never look twice at walking down the street. He was painfully thin, not what you would call good looking at all. He was an auto mechanic and yet he could be in a room of women and at the end of ten minutes every woman in the room would be around him. He had the most marvelous personality. He was witty and funny, and he obviously liked women for women.

He also liked women for sex.

What are some of your fantasies that you have lived out?
For a long time I had the fantasy of making it with someone
I couldn't see, like someone in back of me in a very tight
crowd, or in an elevator stalled between floors and it is all
dark and I couldn't see who it was.

I once met a guy over the phone and we decided to get
together. We met at a hotel. I called him before I left my
house and he told me his room number. He left the key for
me under the mat and told me to knock on the door to give
him a chance to hide in the bathroom. Then, he wanted me
to come inside, take off all my clothes and put on a blindfold.
When I arrived at his room, we argued through the door. I
didn't think I could really do it and he kept telling me to
trust him and do it anyway. I finally decided to live out this
fantasy. We had talked at such length and in such detail over
the months that I knew I had to go for it.

It went great. After I put my blindfold on, he came out of
the bathroom and we started fooling around. We talked for a
while. I asked him if I could take the blindfold off and he
wouldn't let me. After a while, things got hotter and by the
time I knew it, it was over and the blindfold was off. It was
so hot. I don't think I have anything at all to compare it to in
my life. That is the married man I am still seeing after two
years.

Do you ever like to tie up your men?
No, I am the one who likes to be tied up. We have been
talking about experimenting with pain. I bought him a whip
for Christmas and I told him I want him to use it on me.
Since we live in different towns we only get to see each other
about once a month.

Does he spank you?

Not yet, but it has been discussed. We are really new to the bondage scene. The episode in the hotel was the first situation that even remotely resembles that arena. Over the months we have progressed very slowly.

What is the bridge between having fantasies and acting them out?

Having men around that I trust is a big one. The kind of man I trust knows better than to go out and tell everybody in the neighborhood. The man cares enough about me to be sure he doesn't hurt me, and goes out of his way to make sure he doesn't hurt me emotionally or physically. I don't think I could ever get into humiliation.

What do you think guys need to know about sex that they don't know?

Men need to know that a lot of times a woman doesn't have to have an orgasm to enjoy sex. When they keep pushing, it becomes a total turn-off and she'll never be able to come. There is nothing worse to be in the moment and enjoying every sensation and then have someone ask you if you have come or not.

Men need to know that an orgasm achieved through oral sex, manual penetration or finger stimulation is as enjoyable as one achieved through intercourse. Men should not feel or make a woman feel that she is lacking something if that is the only way she can get off.

How many lovers have you had?

Between 120 and 150. The number is even more unusual because I've had so few one night stands.

Name:	**Fiona**
Age:	**50**
Occupation:	**Middle school guidance counselor**
Relationship Status:	**Has a boyfriend**

Are you currently in a relationship?

I'm currently in three relationships.

What qualities do you look for in men you are in relationship with?

I think the most important things are that the person be honest and willing to communicate. I'm not really hung up on looks. I also like maturity. I am not all that picky.

What has inspired you to date so many men?

It wasn't until my children went off to college that I started dating. The freedom opened me up to new experiences. Before that I didn't date at all.

Are you attracted to aggressive sex?

Yes, I am a submissive.

When did it become clear to you that you were submissive?

I think I've known for a long, long time. I never acted on it before and it used to scare me terribly. I have been aware of it since I was a child. I can remember seeing Dale Evans, Roy Rogers' wife, tied up and being very interested and excited by that. I was younger than ten. As I got older I had fantasies of being tied up.

Being hurt is not that big of a deal to me. I get whipped sometimes, but that is more of a punishment. I enjoy some of the whipping. I like being held down, but not serious pain.

Do you have rape fantasies?
Yes I do, but I don't really want that to happen.

What are some fantasies that you haven't yet explored?
The fantasies I have now are more with groups. I want to go to some of the clubs where they have D&S activity, where you can be tied up in public and things like that.

What would it take for that to happen?
The opportunity for it to occur. My master is trying to arrange some meetings for us with other couples and so far only one of them has worked out. We had one meeting with another dominant and submissive couple and we didn't do a whole lot at that meeting. Since then, I've had a lot of fantasies about what else could happen with them. We're going to see them again soon.

What is the most outrageous sexual act you have done?
I've done a lot of things with my master that no one else would do with me. For example, he built a box for me. He likes to make things for me. He puts me into this wooden box. My head sticks out of it. I am also tied up inside the box. He puts vibrators and nipple clamps on me while I am inside the box. Then, he can sit on the box and have me suck him.

How big is the box?
It is big enough for me. I can't stand up inside it. I have to sit down and I am scrunched up. It is not really that uncomfortable.

Do you enjoy talking during sex?
I like to talk, but master doesn't always let me talk.

Do you do phone sex with men?

In the past I was into it. I don't do that a whole lot now because I do real sex most of the time. A year ago when I got started in all this, I did lots of phone sex.

I've interviewed several women who had very straight lives sexually, and then when they got to be around 50 they got into more experimental sex. Why do you think this is?

For me, it is because when women get older they have more freedom. Even if I wanted to do this when my kids were around, I wouldn't have done it because of them being there. I wouldn't want any chance of them seeing it. I just didn't feel free to do so. With this type of sex there is always a chance of being hurt. I have been suspended in the air and I was scared about being dropped.

What would your dream lover be like?

My lover would be like a master, but also very loving. He would dominate me in a very loving way. He would do some bondage, but it would all be very loving. He would actually have sex with me, which my dom refuses to do because he is married. To him, he would cross the line if he actually had intercourse with me, but he doesn't see what he is doing as being wrong.

Sexpectations

Conclusion

I hope that *Sexpectations* has opened up the world of sex to you, and that it has shown you new possibilities and new ways of thinking about sex and dating. At the very least, I hope that this book has shot a few holes in the myth that women don't like sex. The truth is that sex is a natural expression for everyone.

Some people consider "alternative" sex practices to be sick or perverted. This book has tried to open the human side of alternative sex by presenting the thoughts, feelings, and rationales behind the actions. You have heard the words from the women themselves, who clearly believe that what they are doing is safe, sane and consensual.

Considering the powerful antisocial stigma attached to women sharing sexuality, the women I interviewed were very generous in sharing their experiences and entrusting their secrets with us. It is a rare gift to have such honest and candid stories collected in one book.

This is a book about sexual freedom. It may give you permission to fantasize and experiment in ways you never allowed yourself to enjoy before. By exposing readers to a wide variety of fantasies and desires, it will hopefully decrease feelings of alienation and condemnation.

Sexpectations presents a world in which nothing in the realm of fantasy is taboo. Sexuality can be a safe refuge where all of our fantasies to be explored. It can be a space to explore our deepest thoughts and hidden desires. Sexuality can bring out the most juicy, intimate, and personal aspects of ourselves. The path is open to each of us, and it leads to a place where our whole personalities can bloom. Thanks for walking it with me.

Glossary of Terms

BDSM—Bondage, discipline and sadomasochism.

B&D—Bondage and discipline.

Bestiality—The act of having sexual relations with animals.

Bottom- A person who becomes aroused by being sensually controlled by a dominant.

D&S—Dominance and submission.

Dominant, (or Top)—A person who enjoys sexual control over another person.

Dominatrix—A sexually dominant woman, often a professional.

Lifestyle—People who consider BDSM as a crucial part of their lives. For them, it is much more than a "spice" in the bedroom.

Masochist—A person who erotically enjoys receiving pain.

Master—A male dominant.

Mistress—A female dominant.

Power Exchange—The consensual act of a submissive surrendering to a dominant.

S/M—Sadomasochism. Refers to activities where people give and/or receive pain.

Sadist—A person who erotically enjoys hurting others.

Safe Word—A word or expression which stops BDSM play. This is used as a safety mechanism to stop a scene if the submissive feels they cannot continue with a scene because of too much pain, they don't feel safe, or any other reasons.

Scene—The expression "scene" can have two meanings. The first meaning refers to a single erotic episode, usually involving BDSM. The second meaning refers to "the scene." This includes the community of people involved in BDSM and similar communities.

Session—A single BDSM experience. It often refers to professional dominance.

Slave—Refers to a submissive, who enjoys pretending to be owned by a master of mistress. It can also be used a term of affection.

Submissive—A person who is a bottom. A person who likes to be sensually controlled. A person who enjoys submitting to someone else's desires.

Switch—A person who enjoys being both in the role of dominant (sadist) and submissive (masochist). They enjoy "switching" roles.

Vanilla—Usually refers to conventional forms of sexual relations. Also, intimate interactions that do not include D&S or S/M activity.

A Note from the Publisher

We hope you enjoyed *Sexpectations*. This book is part of a series of books which focus on improving all aspects of relationships between men and women. These books address intimacy, sexuality, power, communication, and gender reconciliation. We are proud to have *Sexpectations* as part of this series.